CHARON + MIKE

THANKS FOR ALL [illegible]

AND YOUR UNDERSTAND[illegible]

HAVE BECOME GREAT FRIENDS.

HAVE AN OPEN DOOR IN VAIL

THE CHEF

TOP CHEFS IN TEXAS

Recipes from Celebrated "Toques" With a Touch of Texas

SARAH JANE ENGLISH

EAKIN PRESS ★ Austin, Texas

FIRST EDITION

Published in the United States of America
By Eakin Press
An Imprint of Eakin Publications, Inc.
P.O. Drawer 90159 ★ Austin, TX 78709-0159

ISBN 0-89015-756-1

Library of Congress Cataloging-in-Publication Data

English, Sarah Jane.
Top chefs in Texas: recipes from celebrated "toques" with a touch of Texas/Sarah Jane English.
p. cm.
ISBN 0-89015-756-1 : $15.95
1. Cookery. 2. Cookery — Texas. 3. Wine and wine making. I. Title.
TX714.E54 1990
641.5 — dc20 89-29917
CIP

To my children, Linda Jane and Trey, whose hearty appetites and discriminating tastes inspired me early on.

And to the chefs, for their incredible culinary gifts and participation in Top Chefs.

Other books by Sarah Jane English:

Vin Vignettes

The Wines of Texas

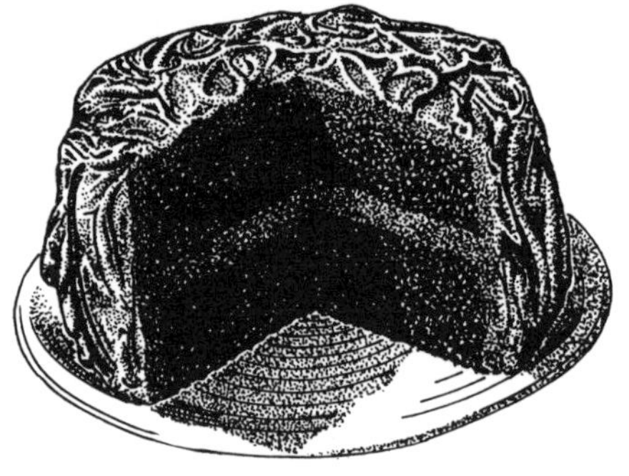

Contents

A History of the Toque

Initially, this book was entitled *Top Toques in Texas;* however, finding that not many people knew that "toque" meant the chef's cap, we decided not to gamble with misunderstanding. Nevertheless, the original idea led the author through a merry, investigative maze of the toque's history.

At one time, it seems, toques were fashionable hats for both men and women to wear. They were small and brimless, or had only a small brim, and fit closely to the head. The word appeared in several languages (French *toque,* Italian *tocca,* and Spanish *toca*) during the sixteenth century and was defined generally as "a small cap or bonnet worn by men and women in various countries" (OED). Many paintings by Hans Holbein the Younger depict toques of varied styles, including the portraits of Erasmus and Henry VIII, whose toque had a soft, full crown pleated into a headband. Often they were made of velvet and other luxurious fabrics, were decorated with gold, beads, and fur and sported a plume.

The toque of the chef, however, has been traced to the Byzantine Empire (*Foods of the Western World* by Theodora Fitzgibbon): "A Greek term, *polita,* was used in culinary contexts to describe urbane cookery originating in Byzantium or cookery in the style for which Constantinople was renowned. During the era of the Byzantine Empire, Constantinople was noted for its culinary achievements. Constantinople is even said to be the place of origin of the chef's white hat (toque). The story runs that after the fall of Constantinople the much-valued imperial chefs took refuge in the monasteries, where they continued to practice their art, greatly to the pleasure of the monks. At first the cooks adopted the black habit and high black hat of the Greek Church, but after a time they felt that their clothes should differ from those of the true monks, and obtained permission to wear the same habit, but in white. Thus the high black hat of the monk became the high white hat of the chef, and it has survived to this day."

Upon my request, my friend Barbara Lang, who teaches at the Cornell University School of Hotel Administration, asked a colleague about the toque. Accordingly, she was told that the 180 folds of the chef's toque represent the 180 different ways one can prepare eggs; however, the instructor could not remember her source.

Preface

The chefs included in *Top Chefs in Texas* do not exhaust the field of capable chefs in Texas, but they give a good indication of the excellent cuisine now available across the Lone Star State. They came to my attention because of their reputations, and I have been privileged to taste their extraordinary preparations.

Six of the chefs have been voted "Who's Who in Food and Wine in Texas." The awards were organized and managed by the *Dallas Morning News*. Five hundred persons from throughout Texas in related industries selected the winners, and staff members of the Texas Department of Agriculture and North Texas State University tabulated the results. *Dallas Morning News* food editor Dotty Griffith issues the awards at the Texas Hill Country Wine and Food Festival in Austin. Other chefs included in this book have received numerous awards and honors.

Additionally, for this book, names of top chefs were submitted by food editors of major newspapers and magazines throughout the state, food critics out of state, and Texas chefs themselves. Several mentions were necessary for inclusion.

Recipes are as distinctive as signatures. In order to preserve the chef's unique manner of expression, I tampered with the recipes as little as possible. Reading them as submitted is a perusal of personality; it makes the book versatile and interesting.

Each chef's collection of recipes constitutes a menu (appetizers, soups, salads, main courses, and desserts) that the reader can cook in her or his own kitchen. Consequently, I invite readers to prepare a feast at home complete with the appropriate wines, duplicating with their own personal touch the delights available at some of Texas's best eateries. If while reading the recipes, however, the home cook is overcome with hunger, the restaurant may be only a short drive or plane trip away.

Lest you think cooking perfection is in the fate of the stars, these top chefs have birthdays in every month of the year. Ten of them were born in the U.S. (only two in Texas), four in Germany, two in France, two in Britain, and one in the Netherlands. The average age is thirty-five, and the average hours per week in the kitchen are sixty-three.

The chefs kindly prepared their recipes for me so that I might select appropriate wines to complement the dishes. My recommendations accompany each recipe. If your taste preference is identical to mine, you're set. If (as is much more likely) you have your own preferences, my suggestions serve as a few of any number of selections. In any event, trust your palate.

In a separate section, all the wines mentioned in the book are listed conveniently for easy perusal. I tasted specific vintages, of course, but I've made suggestions in the chapter on wine and food pairing about adjusting the vintages as the book and wines age.

In Texas, as elsewhere, many of our chefs are graduates of culinary institutes, cooking schools, and rigorous apprenticeships. They have learned classical methods that they have assimilated, revised, and adapted to their own cuisines. A dominant leading but not exclusive force was Southwestern cuisine. Proponents such as Anne Lindsay Greer, Dean Fearing, and Stephan Pyles led in the field. Many talented chefs continue to make contributions to various styles of cuisine, and Texas is the better for it.

The chefs in this book are (listed alphabetically): Bruce Auden, Jeff Blank, Norbert Brandt, Thierry Burklé, Robert Del Grande, Dean Fearing, Victor Gielisse, Anne Lindsay Greer, Lori and David Holben, Timothy Keating, Joe Mannke, Robert McGrath, Bruce Molzan, Daniel O'Leary, Michel Bernard Platz, Elmar Prambs, Stephan Pyles, Gert Rausch, and Andrew Thomson. Their example has set a standard for other great chefs to follow.

Acknowledgments

My deep gratitude to all the fabulously talented chefs. Thank you for writing and testing the recipes and for all your cooperation in helping to make this book a reality. Thank you, too, Donna Derryberry, Alison Williams, Maggi Jones, Melinda James, Gaye Tullos, Royal Rowe, Clive O'Donoghue, and Mike Murphy.

Thank you Marvin Overton for friendship, time, and expertise.

Thank you Chef Paul Bocuse for your research on toques (chef's hat) and support of my efforts.

Thank you Lloyd Mardis for helping with research and sharing ideas about design.

Thank you Linda Jane Rylee for proofing the manuscript.

Thank you Mollie Sharpe and Jean Gilbert for reviewing the recipes.

Thank you Barbara Lang for your information on research for toques.

Foreword: Paul Bocuse Comments

Chef Paul Bocuse and I became acquainted in Dallas at the Crescent Court over a delicious lunch created by Chef Dan O'Leary. We visited about food and he shared his ideas with me. In the form I've listed them below, they resemble Brillat-Savarin's "Aphorisms," only in my opinion, with greater heartfelt philosophy. Additionally, Bocuse believes that young French chefs should come to the United States to see what is happening here.

"American chefs such as yours in Texas are becoming esteemed today," Bocuse said. "Several years ago one never knew the name of the chef in this country, or rarely so. Through the years it has been very hard work to get recognition. Now the names of chefs are as big as any celebrity. Cooking, however, is hard work, and it is important to keep the proper perspective and not let the publicity go to your head.

"What has changed as much as the quality of the cooking is the quality of the ingredients," Bocuse said. "Twenty years ago, when I came to this country to cook, there was not much available to buy. I had to bring this with me. I could not buy shallots, many types of fish, truffles, caviar, and so forth. It is very different today."

Bocuse is a charming and sensitive man of a generous nature and *tres* gifted with culinary talent. He autographed for me a copy of the menu from his restaurant in Collonges au Mont d'Or, France, and I autographed for him a copy of my first book, *Vin Vignettes*. Then, in the fashion of true French friends, we kissed on both cheeks and parted smiling, looking forward to a reunion.

Aphorisms of Paul Bocuse

1. Art nourishes the soul. Therefore, a great artist is greater than a great chef. The goal of a chef is to bring happiness and contentment, but he shouldn't believe his own importance too much.
2. The greatest chef who has only mediocre ingredients will have a very difficult time creating a dish, but a mediocre chef with great ingredients can prepare excellent dishes.
3. Every time you cook it is an adventure. You never know exactly how the preparation will finish.
4. A chef should never be too confident.
5. With music the score is always written down, so someone with even a little talent can play. But to cook you have to have that sixth sense of what is needed — what has to be added — to make it the perfect dish.
6. It is most important for chefs to share enthusiasm. A chef hopes the techniques are learned, but it is of the utmost importance to smile at those on the line who are cutting the carrots and peeling potatoes day after day.
7. One should cook for friends. It is impossible to cook a good meal for people you don't like.
8. Sometimes it is nicer to cook for those unaccustomed to fine dining. They are so pleased and grateful.
9. I prefer to cook fish. There are so many different kinds and the variations are limitless.
10. Bland cheeses are great foils for other flavors.
11. Good flavors are always related.
12. A country that produces wine is necessarily a better country for food.
13. The best cooking technique is to have fresh products of the best quality. (I have three full-time gardeners tending my herbs and produce.) It also helps to have a quality chef.

Part I

The Dining Experience

1.

A Fine Dining Overview: Then and Now

This book was the most brilliant idea I've ever had. Just imagine traveling from city to city to have celebrated chefs prepare dinner for you in order to select an appropriate wine. Brilliant!

The process has been an enormous amount of fun and interestingly varied. Sometimes the chef would prepare the courses and then bring each one out for us to enjoy together. Often I dined alone and was given the recipes to study. Other times the co-owner, some other principal, or my daughter would join me. In every instance, the occasion was pure delight.

One evening I was dining alone and had the opportunity to observe several tables around me, all occupied by couples. One couple was celebrating a twenty-fifth wedding anniversary. He had given her a corsage of red roses and baby's breath which overwhelmed her tiny shoulder. They exchanged comments about the day with unusual attention toward each other, and evident affection as they toasted their love with glasses of wine. At another table a politician in his sixties was trying to woo a lady friend of long standing with an incredibly boyish approach, perhaps to accentuate the longtime crush he had endured. Imagine attempting that without a mellowing glass of wine. In the other direction a man dazzled his date with his feats in the business world. Brother, what an operator! He had selected a nice Cabernet Sauvignon to assist his performance.

Wine experiences can be special as well as memorable. In Houston at Cafe Annie, Chef Robert Del Grande and I compared several wines to see how they tasted with various dishes. We were surprised to discover how well the Rutherford Hills 1985 Merlot went with a salad of romaine, mango, and sweet peppers with cream dressing and a dry cheese. We had expected the wine to be too big, but it wasn't. Chef Del Grande prepared my first course and then instructed the sous chef thereafter so he could join me for the rest of the dinner. I felt *really* special when his wife Mimi told me he never left his kitchen like that. But what a clever man, and so entertaining. After earning his Ph.D. in biochemistry, he took time off to work in the restaurant kitchen of a friend. Now he owns it.

Executive Chef Elmar Prambs prepares some of the most absolutely elegant food in Texas at the Four Seasons Hotel Riverside Cafe in Austin. He and Royal Rowe, food and beverage director, and I shared our numerous courses, or rather, I ate mine and they shared theirs with me. The Lobster Ravioli with Tomato Butter Sauce and Chives is to kill for! The Kendall-Jackson 1987 Chardonnay and the Flora Springs 1984 Cabernet Sauvignon both complemented the dish superbly.

Another dish worthy to set before kings is Chef Stephan Pyles's Tamale Tart with Roasted Garlic Custard and Fresh Lumped Crabmeat. It's wonderful to watch Stephan work. He touches all the ingredients, almost caressing them in order to know them more thoroughly. And he smells everything too. I understand the practice. I smell my glasses of wine just as often. After all, olfactory is responsible for eighty-five percent of what is tasted. In the case of the Tamale Tart, I liked both the Ferrari-Carano 1987 Fumé Blanc and Chardonnay. The Chardonnay better suits the richness of the custard, but Sauvignon Blanc complements the crabmeat and enhances the flavors of the tart. Treat yourself to both bottles.

I never thought anyone could make me eat flowers, but edible flowers are the specialty of Chef Michel Bernard Platz and with his magic touch, I would be inclined to eat almost anything. I must say the exquisite Roederer Estate sparkling wine goes equally well with all flowers. Chef Platz waves his wand over L'Entrecote at the Loews Anatole in Dallas. What an exquisite dining experience it is to be served with Baccarat crystal, Italian silver flatware, and handsome china. Ah, these are the good old days.

And Cafe Pacific is really terrific with Chef Andrew Thomson. I think I've eaten most of the dishes on the menu and everything has been superb. He is endowed with the unique ability to have crisp things remain crisp and succulent things remain succulent. These textures frequently have a way of reversing themselves once placed on a plate, but not on Andrew's plates. The Tortilla Salad is a perfect example and the Sterling 1987 Sauvignon Blanc is a nice complement.

Holland lost a national treasure when Victor Gielisse became a Texan. What an artist this master chef is! His creative combinations are pure melting poetry, and superlatives roll off the tongue so readily after one of his incomparable dishes that the diner is transformed into a poet as well. The Fresh Fruit Cobbler is like no other you'll ever eat.

Victor also poses some challenges. One recipe, Seafood Sausage, reflects the classic style of Escoffier. It begins: "prepare forcemeat." Escoffier's recipes often read similarly; for example, a recipe for duck might instruct: "find an excellent duck; prepare it to perfection." I requested a recipe for forcemeat and Victor most obligingly complied. He was delightful to work with and so accommodating. The sausages are well worth the effort and beautifully accompanied by the Beaulieu 1988 Dry Sauvignon Blanc.

A marvel of all marvels is Anne Lindsay Greer, not only for her extraordinary cooking ability but also because she is extraordinarily petite. *Cook's* magazine recorded that Anne "helped spread jalapeño pasta and cilantro pesto from coast to coast," and consequently has become known as "the high priestess of innovative Southwestern cooking." Some years ago, Anne invited Dean Fearing and Stephan Pyles initially, and then Robert Del Grande a bit later, to discuss their mutual cooking interests. Those conversations evolved into the creation of Southwestern cuisine. Her recipes are like a litany of praises to the products of the grill, and so, of course, to her.

Extremely casual, the brassy, bistro-style Ruggles Grill Chef Bruce Molzan nonetheless offers some of the finest dining I've eaten anywhere in Texas. With his flawless concentration on selecting foods, Molzan focuses on dressing his fish in deliciously light herb crusts (see recipe) and other delectable covers for the freshest bounty from the sea. His wife Susan is responsible for the desserts, and she certainly does herself proud. Try two or three.

Acclaim and medals come easily to my retinue of chefs, but Robert McGrath overreacted. He has won twenty-six gold medals for his culinary efforts. We enjoyed dining together on, at last count, fifteen of his menu items. I was in heaven! And Chef McGrath seemed mildly pleased himself. He treats his kitchen like a nursery where each dish is his offspring. Everything looked and tasted perfectly prepared.

As my little narrative reveals, *Top Chefs in Texas* was a most rewarding idea. In any event, and perhaps in every respect, these chefs epitomize fine food, while wine accentuates the "fine" in dining.

To prove the above point, I pose a couple of questions. At White House dinners, have you heard of heads of state toasted with buttermilk? And would a ship be truly christened with lemonade instead of Champagne? I don't think so. Fine events call for fine wine. Likewise, a dinner without wine to enhance the food lacks an essential element. Since grapes are food products that ferment naturally, wine is the perfect food beverage. And there's a great deal of pleasure in exploring wines and foods together. As in most things, balance and harmony are consistent with the amount and degree of enjoyment.

I love to eat. Travel abroad, in general, educated American palates, I believe, about fine food and wine. It was certainly my training ground. As a young adult I first traveled to France and recall vividly an elegant dinner in Paris. It was at the renowned La Tour d'Argent. This historic and proper restaurant has great style. Two handsome couples not far from our table ordered an appetizer of chilled caviar. It was brought to the table in the center of a twenty-five-pound block of ice. A window table had been recommended by the authors of *A Parisian's Guide to Paris,* Henri Gault and Christian Millau. They were so right: "From the roof of a building on the banks of the Seine, 385 years of gastronomy contemplate more than eight centuries of faith: the Cathedral of Notre-Dame de Paris, aglow with a thousand lights."

I adored the fact that women were served menus without items being priced. I ordered with abandon. The quenelles of pike followed by duck were superb and my dessert was too — three huge *pâté à choux* puffs filled with vanilla bean ice cream and covered with a warm, rich, freshly made chocolate sauce. The sommelier did not present a wine list. He *was* the wine list. Once he knew what had been ordered, he advised about the wine selection, a happy task to be repeated throughout my visit. Before long I began to realize how well the Volnay of Marquis d'Angerville suited my sautéed veal, or a lovely Château Haut Brion paired with duck, or the Montrachet of Bouchard Père et Fils complemented my fish with a cream sauce and the robustly flavored Château des Jacques of Thorin accompanied braised lamb.

I've traveled annually, and sometimes twice a year, to France since that first trip and never tire of the fine dining experiences. Indeed, there's always the wonderful cuisine of an unknown chef to experience, like Chef Didier Delu of Didier Delu Restaurant, a twelve-table treasure in the fifteenth arrondisement. Now being in Paris wouldn't be the same without one of Didier's fabulous feasts with his perfect *mille-feuille* and the pleasant company of his wife, Sabine.

Fine food, even in Paris, is not always limited to tables with white linen cloths, crystal, and silver flower containers. I remember a delicious Tarte Bourbonnaise with a refreshing Sancerre at a stand-up sidewalk cafe near the Place de L'Opera. But neither the wine nor the cheese tart could be found back in Texas. So my trips abroad have been essentially a search for fine food and wine. In 1970 I took my ten-year-old son to share many of my favorite restaurants and wines (sips only) with him. He fell in love with the fresh Dover sole and at one restaurant amazed the waiter by ordering a second one.

But such infrequent visits hardly satisfy wine and food enthusiasts. Also, the trips are often too short to really absorb everything. And frequently the names of wines are too difficult to pronounce or remember (one of the reasons I wrote *Vin Vignettes*). At first, like others, I brought the labels home with me and stocked some familiar vintages. The more famous bottles were readily available. When I requested a bottle that was not in stock, another similar in style would be recommended. I offered my friends wine instead of bourbon and branch water and they became accustomed to the habit in my home. I read wine books by the dozens and my wine knowledge and vocabulary increased. Still, I longed for the quality and diversity of the dishes I'd enjoyed in France but couldn't find in Texas, so I collected cookbooks, learned to prepare the food, and served it at home with wine. My family loved it!

There were, however, some interesting repercussions. It was my habit to take my daughter and son to an enchanting playground each Saturday morning. They would ride miniature red tractors around bales of hay and a miniature red barn; float in small boats on a constructed canal; soar in little helicopters on an up and down motored device; and enjoy several other fun diversions especially built for small children. Afterwards we went to a hamburger place for lunch. We'd sit at the counter and order milk shakes, French fries, and hamburgers. One Saturday after I had begun my "gourmet" cooking, my son surprised the waitress by ordering Coq au Vin and Chocolate Mousse. The waitress, a crusty replica of the television character Alice, put her pencil behind her ear, fluffed her pocket handkerchief, leaned on her elbow, and asked, "Here or to go?" Home cooking took on a whole new meaning to my son, but my daughter was the real adventurer, always eager to try new foods — regardless of how pungent.

Then, in the 1970s, came the American wine revolution (about the same time Alice Waters opened Chez Panisse and started the gastronomic revolution). Following closely was the rejuvenation of the Texas wine industry and Anne Lindsay Greer's influence on Southwestern cuisine. It established a unique style of food with a region that was chic. Texas and things Texan — boots, big belts, jeans, Stetsons, and barbecue — were all the rage. These events gave rise to another phenomenon — the celebrity chef. Again, wine accentuated the "fine" in dining. More people were traveling abroad and having fine dining experiences, frequently in the hotels where they stayed. Hotel dining became synonymous with fine food and wine. Back home in Texas, Caroline Rose Hunt supplied the missing gap with her Rosewood hotels in Dallas and Houston, hotels with three of my top chefs and a nice selection of wines.

At the same time, a pronounced change was happening with the way food and entertainment were perceived in Texas. Before, during and after the war years, throughout the 1950s, and into the 1960s, fine dining in Texas, with exceptions, occurred in the home, or at a country club or some other private club. "Eating out" was on Thursdays, the cook's day off, and the family treated the children to barbecue, Mexican food, Chinese food, or other favorites not usually served at home. Generally, the place was a family restaurant in the neighborhood.

But the 1970s were different. Household servants were a thing of the past. Working mothers occupied the kitchen and shortcuts were necessary. Cold cereals and Pop-tarts replaced hot oatmeal with butter and cream and eggs and bacon, reinforced by the health boom and low-cholesterol diets. As women left the kitchen in increasing numbers to find significance in a career outside the home, eating out became an established habit. The trend accelerated. Women began to order a glass of white wine instead of a cocktail. It was the precursor of the elaborate selection of wines now offered by the glass.

At the same time, healthful diets became a big issue. Wine suited the moderate consumption prescription as well as the healthful issue. Wines became a matter of supply and demand.

The culinary world took notice. In Texas, as elsewhere, apprenticed chefs and graduates of cooking schools learned practical and classical methods that were respected and adapted to their own cuisines. For the first time, America was producing major chefs with impressive skills in large numbers. A dominant leading force was Southwestern cuisine. Proponents such as Anne Lindsay Greer, Dean Fearing, and Stephan Pyles led the field of the many talented chefs who continue to make contributions. As a consequence, a standard was created, and with the model firmly launched, other chefs follow.

The heritage of fine dining is not as old as one might think. It once belonged only to royalty. Possibly the first great French chef was Taillevent, head cook for Charles VI in the fourteenth century. His cookbook, *Viandier,* ranks as one of the oldest in France (circa 1375). By the end of the sixteenth century, the position of chef was established as an extremely important and significant one. In France, lavish platters with huge amounts of beautifully presented food were paraded before the king. It was not unusual to find 150 or more items on the menu. Prior to the late eighteenth century, the art of great chefs was a patronage occupation reserved for the noble classes. One event, the French Revolution, changed that disposition entirely. Hundreds of chefs were forced underground. One of them, Beauvilliers, had the bright idea of showing his dedication to democracy by opening a restaurant that offered the dishes he had prepared for his patrons. The revolutionaries embraced the idea enthusiastically and ate their way to his success.

At the time of the French Revolution there were only about fifty restaurants in Paris, and they owed their existence to an emerging practice of the period. During the eighteenth century it became very fashionable to entertain with intimate suppers, called *petite soupers* because often they began with a tureen of rich soup. In Paris, restaurants featuring these luscious liquids began to open. Consequently, soup gets the credit for establishing the first restaurant as well as the word "restaurant" itself. In 1765, an enterprising soup vendor, Monsieur Boulanger, began offering at his restaurant, Champs Oiseau, a menu of "magical restaurants" — that is, restoratives (soups) that revived and invigorated. Not only was his business successful, but his soups became the rage of Paris.

Brillat-Savarin loved to dine and adored the best of its kind of anything. He wrote the *Physiologie du Gout* (1825), which expresses his ideas on taste, gastronomy, the senses, appetite, thirst, drink, and other subjects. His aphorisms are legendary: "Beasts feed: man eats: the man of intellect alone knows how to eat"; "Gourmandism is an act of judgment, by which we give preference to things which are agreeable to our taste over those which have not that quality"; "Tell me what you eat and I'll tell you what you are." His work is a precise prescription for a proper gourmet.

Another well-known food personality of the early nineteenth century was Chef Carême. The expression of his talents were shared by two noteworthies of the time, Talleyrand, the foreign minister of Louis XVIII, and Czar Alexander I of Russia. Carême's tradition was also La Grande Cuisine, which might include twenty-five or more courses.

In the late nineteenth century, however, Escoffier dominated the culinary scene. His thoughts were first published in his *Le Guide Culinaire* (1902). It is still considered the standard reference for professionals and illustrates how a few courses, three or four, can satisfy with contrasts, balancing flavors, and weights, textures and richness — the same considerations that apply to wines, which indeed, he included as part of the meal. His consideration was for the palate, to keep it fresh and stimulated, surprised and excited throughout a meal. With Escoffier, and his followers, a meal became an integrated expression. Simplicity became art.

In the first half of the twentieth century, the man of the hour was Fernand Point. His restaurant, La Pyramide, was considered extraordinary, even among those having obtained the Michelin three-star designation. During his tenure he acquired the unique reputation for training the most chefs who received France's premier culinary honor, "Great Chefs of France."

A story is told about this master chef and the then president of France, Charles de Gaulle. A question of protocol arose. Would Point go down the steps of his restaurant to meet the president, who clearly should not come up the stairs to a waiting Point? The dilemma was solved when they decided to meet each other halfway.

Point's culinary offsprings include Paul Bocuse (the first French chef to receive the Legion d'Honneur from the French president), Roger Vergé, and Pierre Troisgros, to mention three. Many American chefs have studied under these or other Point graduates, and most of Texas's top chefs have read Escoffier and studied the techniques of classic cuisine as well. And it all began with the French Revolution.

Ideas often promote radical changes. Texans, and indeed Americans, have definitely been in the process of revolutionizing their approach to dining. Of course, we've been inheriting culinary ideas from France and elsewhere for generations. Having wine on the table is one of them. I believe the phenomenon of fine dining is connected to wine. And even though the concept has never disappeared, wine has put "fine" back into dining.

For example, I grew up in Dallas during the 1940s and 1950s, when entertaining and dinner parties were given at home. My family, like many at the time, had a cook to prepare the food and a butler to serve it. Beautiful china, crystal, and silver candelabra were objects to be used and enjoyed, not stored away in some cabinet. Fine linens, lovely table settings, and fingerbowls seemed to educe civility in our dining room, where Champagne was the favorite wine beverage. Holidays were occasions for Sauternes, which we served throughout the meal. Good manners also were preeminent. Even a hint of leaning toward the soup bowl or plate, or talking with food in the mouth, and I was sent immediately from the table. Often today, as I watch Yuppies and their ilk slurping soup with scarcely an inch between the bowl and their mouths, I recall how pleasant it was to show respect and courtesy for those in your company by such simple means as a straight back, eye contact during conversation, and noiseless eating.

In addition to entertaining at home, there were private clubs, like the many country clubs or downtown clubs such as the Dallas Athletic Club and its popular luncheon dish — breast of turkey covered with a rich Thousand Island dressing and served on shredded lettuce and fresh white bread with garnishes. Certainly, there were a few good restaurants, like the Old Warsaw (Chicken a la Kiev was a favorite) and Mario's (pasta dishes and huge filets of tenderloin with baked potatoes). These restaurants were owned by first-generation immigrants who recreated the food they had enjoyed in their homelands but adapted to Texans' taste for beef.

More often than not, entertaining away from home took place in one of the landmark, elegant hotels — the Baker or the Adolphus. I vividly remember my birthday parties in the exciting Century Room at the Adolphus. An orchestra played popular songs in the evening for those wanting to dance. Then, during showtime, the dance floor receded under the bandstand to reveal an ice arena for the beautiful skaters who performed for our delight. Afterwards, or before, such famous personalities as Bob Hope or Jack Benny, Hildegarde or Liberace would appear. My sister Nancy and I wore long evening dresses and were given corsages on these occasions. Nancy always began with a shrimp cocktail while I selected fresh fruit. Dinners were generally four courses: the appetizer, a soup or salad, the main course, and dessert. The Adolphus pastry chef was a marvel, a Belgian who ushered the art of ice sculpting, made authentic French breads, and introduced me to my first Napoleon, still a favorite. We were even permitted a taste of Champagne.

The Century Room era, with its fabulous Ice Revues, lobster, prime ribs, and pastries, lasted from 1936 to 1965. Newer hotels with better arrangements and facilities for meetings and conventions, especially those of the garment industry, began moving to Dallas and soon dominated. Mall locations also were competitive to downtown. Grand balls, galas, and expense accounts seemed to substitute for the small, more intimate dinners and special occasions. In time, the Baker was demolished for another structure to be built on its important land and the Adolphus underwent a complete restoration to reopen in 1981 as a Texas Historic Landmark.

In 1949 Neiman Marcus published a cookbook titled *A Taste of Texas*. The recipes were culled from 2,000 received from the store's customers. The book included the "best and most interesting dishes served by prominent Texans at home, at parties, wherever good food and good cheer combine to embellish life": Tyrone Power's "Eggs Benedict"; Lilly Dache's "Pate, By Dache"; Elizabeth

Arden's "Caviar Canape"; "Frijoles a la Dobie" from J. Frank Dobie, and so forth. Home entertaining remained a major format after World War II.

There were attitudinal inheritances from the war years too. Food shortages, substitutes, oleomargarine instead of butter, frozen orange juice instead of fresh, and so forth, brought new perceptions from necessities. Not the least of new considerations was food programs on television. Early in the next decade Julie Bennell, food editor of the *Dallas Morning News,* demonstrated on television many of the recipes published in the newspaper. These were quick, easy recipes that often used leftovers and canned soups and vegetables — hardly Brillat-Savarin's idea of fine dining, or mine, but nonetheless popular with a large segment of the postwar society.

Then a really refreshing and bright star came on the Texas scene during the mid-1950s, Helen Corbitt. Before moving on to the Zodiac Room at Neiman Marcus, she directed the kitchen at the Driskill Hotel in Austin. "Hot Turkey Mornay with Fresh Broccoli" was the most popular dish on the Sunday luncheon menu, but she offered so much more — lots of fresh herbs, heavy cream, sauces, and wine. She set the standard for rich tastes in food. At the Zodiac, Corbitt introduced mounds of lettuce for her fancy chicken salad with grapes and toasted almonds and fresh fruit arrangements, while her creative presentations included an ice cream dessert frozen in a miniature pottery flower pot.

There's another element to the fine dining picture. Experiences abroad during the war years introduced many Americans to fine food and wine. Once those tragic days ended and reconstruction began, tours of duty abroad continued. In the more peaceful times that followed, professors and students studied in foreign countries. Oil companies and other businesses established bases abroad. The exposure to different cultures and their pleasant dining habits left an impression. Many were converted to dining with wine forever after, and a number of restaurateurs were among them.

During the late 1960s, for instance, Norman Eaton opened the glittering Polonaise restaurant atop the Westgate in downtown Austin and ushered in a new type of dining for the capital. There was actually a *carte du vin,* even though Lancer's Rosé dominated most of the wine orders. It was a start. About the same time, a Belgian named André introduced his superb European cuisine, presented in a more provincial setting than the Polonaise, but his cuisine forever spoiled palates accustomed to the usual quotidian fare.

These restaurants and others around the state, as well as dining rooms in luxury hotels, replicated European food styles, service, and presentation. As a matter of fact, elegant hotel dining became synonymous with fine food and wine. French wines were available if often unpronounceable. Then, in the 1970s, California wines gained an international reputation. Stag's Leap and Château Montelena beat their French competitors in a blind tasting in Paris judged by Frenchmen in 1976. At this time in Texas, the modern pioneers were relaunching the Texas wine industry. Many of these winemakers had learned about wines in Europe or California (see Sarah Jane English, *The Wines of Texas*).

Lower air fares, longer vacations, foreign assignments, and greater discretionary income allowed more people to travel, especially abroad, than ever before. Once home, they wanted the same dining experiences. Caroline Rose Hunt responded by opening three of the finest hotels in the world: The Mansion on Turtle Creek in Dallas, The Remington (now Ritz-Carlton) in Houston, and The Crescent Court in Dallas. Ms. Hunt recognized that fine dining was an integral part of an elegant hotel, and Texans agreed. At these hotels and others, travelers could find the same fine dining experiences discovered throughout Europe, and we began to glimpse the advent of an American tradition in the making. Eventually, demand urged the supply, but there were other circumstances as well.

Fewer and fewer persons could afford the extravagant homes or find the servants needed to maintain them. Home entertaining became simplified. Buffet service replaced the white-gloved butler and a series of courses. More women worked and fewer cooked. Restaurants became the cynosures for entertaining. Culinary institutes gained prominence with larger enrollments while universities added classes in oenology. By the 1980s, American regional cuisines were established and were even occasionally being copied abroad. I remember dining in a marvelous little restaurant in St. Emilion during the 1988 harvest and being served a salsa of fresh tomatoes, red onions, peppers, and cilantro with my fish. The classic French techniques are still learned and used, but with evolving variations and innovations.

Today, the wine and food industries are growing together through their mutual support and dependence. In 1985, Susan Auler, co-owner of Fall Creek Vineyards, brought together a group of interested persons to create the Texas Hill Country Wine and Food Festival. I was a charter council and board member and one of a small core group — Susan Auler, Cindy Stone, Tricia Zeigler, Jeannine Stroth — who expended tremendous energy and effort to launch the event in 1986. That year we sent 20,000 invitations, but we wanted them to be personalized. So Susan and I would often meet after dinner to hand address and stamp the invitations, often working past midnight.

"Texas experienced a proliferation of new restaurants in the 1970s," Susan explained, "and simultaneously a Texas wine industry was emerging. I felt the time was right to focus on the exciting new developments in wine and food in Texas. Basically, we wanted to focus on the Hill Country as a viticultural region and additionally on Texas food products, Texas cooking and Texas chefs, hence the first Texas Hill Country Wine and Food Festival was inaugurated in 1986." (The festival benefits KMFA, a non-profit, listener-supported, classical music radio station, and KLRU-TV, a public television station, both in Austin.)

As a fifth-generation Texan, I grew up eating a lot of beef. Roasts and steaks were consumed weekly (still are) and we even grew our own beef on our farm near Garland, now a suburban area called English Estates. Involving the Texas Beef Industry Council in the Hill Country Festival was a natural, and in 1987 it joined our effort to add tremendously to our volunteer effort. Anne Anderson, executive director of the Council, summarized its involvement: "In many ways the festival and the beef industry are good companions. Beef is a trendy food again. It's bred to be leaner and even more healthful. When we promote beef at the festival, the chefs involved come up with new and exciting recipes. Participants come to learn about food and wine, and it's an ideal medium for the modern beef industry."

The year 1988 marked the inauguration of "Who's Who in Food and Wine in Texas." It honored the arrival of Texas personalities who were making noteworthy contributions to the food and wine industries. I was thrilled to be one of the first recipients. As mentioned earlier, six of the chefs included in *Top Chefs in Texas* also are recipients.

Trends continue to shape and change lifestyles and food styles, but I believe fine food and wine will be a constant in the lives of discriminating Texans.

Part II

The Element of Wine

2.

Guidelines in Food-Wine Pairing

Tastes for wine are as specific as tastes for music or art. That is why there are so many different styles. Nonetheless, there are some guidelines for the curious. Remember school days and comparing and contrasting? It's the same with food and wine. Certain foods go with certain wines because they're comparable. Other combinations may have an affinity because of stark contrasts. One of my favorites is peanut butter and Champagne. It's a great late-night snack.

Your preference for flavors and textures is unique. According to Dr. Morley Kare, professor of physiology, who spoke at a Society of Wine Educators Conference, part of your preferences are determined when you're conceived: they are genetic. Besides nature, there's also a nurture side to the comment. What you lack genetically you can acquire from your environment. Tastes are also learned.

The nice thing about pairing wines with foods is that there are no absolutes. Matching wine and food is an art, not a science. Individual tastes govern selections and should rule the decision. Having said that, I would like to point out that chemistry shows why certain combinations of flavors do well together. Even so, the combinations can be altered by adding one significant ingredient.

That's why suggesting a broad category, such as Texas white wine with Gulf Coast fish, is not always effective. There are too many styles of white wines and too many ways to prepare fish. A more acceptable generalized rule is that delicate foods need delicate wines and heartier foods need heftier wines. In addition, textures and weights, and whether items complement one another, are to be considered.

Let's use quail as an example. Quails are inherently sweet meats. They also can carry smoky flavors. For example, quail that is grilled would have a smoky character. Many Texas chefs believe that choosing one wood over another, say a pecan rather than a mesquite, can alter the smoke flavor. In any event, sweet meat with a smoky flavor goes well with a Chenin Blanc or a Riesling with a hint of residual sugar. A crisply roasted quail filled with herbal stuffing would be better served with a crisp Sauvignon Blanc. Marinating the bird in a berry/wine marinade adds fruity flavors that would better match a fruity Merlot or Carneros Pinot Noir.

In any event, wine selections are influenced by the cooking methods, sauces, stuffings, or marinades used. Of course, there are some people who are going to drink red wine with everything because they like only red wines. The same is true of white wine drinkers. That's fine. I don't believe wine and food pairings should ever be too precise.

Chemically, wine contains more than several hundred compounds with estimates ranging up to 2,000. They combine to give flavors and odors to wine. Olfactory is responsible for eighty-five percent or more of what you taste. Of all the constituents, acidity has prime significance. Acid is probably the most important consideration in determining which wines go with which foods. For some reason, crisp acidity works with food. Wines with crisp acids highlight the flavors in foods.

There are some don'ts. Don't try to use wines high in alcohol with food. Big, robust Zinfandels are difficult to match with food. High alcohol Cabernet Sauvignons, even though they are smooth and mellow and have preserved their fruit, need to be matched carefully with certain types of food. An exception that does pair well would be fortified wines, like a Port with Stilton or sweet Late Harvest wines with *foie gras*. High alcohol, unless balanced by sweetness, kills flavors.

Low alcohol, acidity, and texture combine in some wines to

make them the best choices with food, such as Buena Vista Gamay Beaujolais and other light fruity red wines, Geyser Peak Soft Johannisberg Riesling or Fall Creek Emerald Riesling, Hacienda or a Grand Cru Chenin Blanc, or white table wines like Llano Estacado Heritage White Table Wine.

Foods prepared as sweet dishes can be very difficult to match with wines. For example, duck with sweetened and spicy fruit sauces. This is one area where blush wines often work. Likewise, dishes that are too hot with spices make wine pairing difficult. Some Thai and Southwestern foods contain such hot peppers and spices that the only suitable beverage, in my opinion, is Pepto Bismol. Such spices ruin the palate. In the case of Mexican food, I prefer a sparkling wine or a riesling. Sparkling wines clean and refresh the palate. Rieslings with residual sugar, or other similarly styled wines, calm the heat of spices.

There are also misconceptions. Serving the same wine used to prepare a dish does not guarantee a good match. Also, the spiciest wine — Gewurztraminer is an example — does not necessarily go well with the spiciest foods.

Remember, suggested pairings of food and wine are not culinary imperatives but merely suggestions. There are no certainties in this art form. With that in mind, I offer some suggestions.

INGREDIENTS

This list gives an idea about the characteristics in foods we use with meats, fish, and fowl (the major consideration in selecting a wine for a one-wine meal) in order to help in choosing a wine. Match wines with similar or different characteristics.

wild rice — nutty, earthy, a neutral food
poblano sauce — spicy, vegetable, acid
garlic — strong, pungent, sharp, distinctive
parsley — green herbal, mild, fresh
black pepper — strong, hot, sharp, spicy
onions — sweet, sour, strong
mustard — strong, hot, acid, pungent
mushroom — earthy, musty, neutral food
grilling — smoky, sweet, spicy
apple — sweet, acid, fruity
sage — distinctive, herbal, dusty, pungent

lemon — sharp, acid, citrus, sour
rosemary — herbal, floral
bacon — sweet, pungent, oily, strong
dill — herbal, floral
cucumber — vegetable, acid, pungent
curry — distinctive, sharp, perfumy
coconut — sweet, nutty, rich, creamy
almond — nutty, rich, crunchy
butter — rich, fatty, mellow, smooth
hot pepper — acid, pungent, sharp, distinctive
cream and cheese — rich, fatty, smooth, pungent or sweet
spinach — greenness, acid, vegetative, sharp, tannic
fennel — licorice, sharp, bitter, pungent
eggplant — sharp, acid, smooth, bitter
potato — mild, textured, neutral food
carrot — sweet, textured
pecans — tannic, sweet, textured

The main acids in wine are tartaric and malic and they're less sour than acetic (vinegar) and citric acids (lemon, etc.). Generally, younger wines have higher acidity than older ones. Both cream and wine have lactic acid. Wines undergoing secondary fermentation have more lactic acid and blend with cream (some Chardonnays, some Sauvignon Blancs, most reds undergo malo-lactic fermentation).

GENERAL STATEMENTS

Foods prepared with abundant butter, and mild, gently flavored foods are the easiest to pair with wine. Butter imparts a mellowness that has a smooth effect on a dish. Chicken cooked simply in butter will go with almost any wine. The same is true for fresh, young veal. Both have understated flavors that make versatile pairings possible.

For those reasons, chicken and veal are easier to pair with wine than lamb, venison, wild boar, exotic game, or other highly flavored dishes — or often even shellfish or fish. In all cases, the simpler the preparation, the easier the pairing.

Consider the similarity of characteristics between food and wine: age and freshness, fruitiness, the spices, smoothness, the herbs, lightness or heaviness, whether it is smoked, butteriness, degrees of complexity in both wine and food and so forth. For example, prepare a lightly flavored, medium-textured fish in butter, lemon, and garlic and serve it with variously styled Sauvignon Blancs: a light Château Souverain or Sterling, a medium-bodied Kendall-Jackson, and a full-bodied Ferrari-Carano or Cakebread. Compare how the wines vary in style with the food and see which you like best. Which wine seems to be lean (not rich), which is the most crisp, which stands up best to the flavors of the garlic and butter, and which seems to be more nearly the same weight as the fish?

Venison or other game prepared with herbs and spices or even just grilled (depending on the age and strong flavors of the meat) calls for a red wine flavored with toasty, smoky aromas and hearty, earthy nuances to complement the dish. Many proprietary wines do nicely with game. Conn Creek, Villa Mt. Eden and Caymus, or any number of fine Cabernet Sauvignon wines, complement game. A Ravenswood or Rodney Strong Zinfandel work well too.

A tightly textured, strong Cabernet Sauvignon can offset the strong flavor of some lamb. A crisp Chardonnay or Sauvignon Blanc can cut through the oiliness in many fishes. Often a wine does not go with fish; generally, red wines frequently make fish taste metallic. Chenin Blancs and Rieslings are good with light, poached fish dishes.

Sometimes food and wine are balanced by letting the flavors and characteristics of each one come through separately but without fighting each other. Dry white wines, like those from Beringer, or even sparkling wines, like those from Domaine Mumm, Domaine Chandon, or Roederer Estate, often work well with smoked fish.

The more difficult foods to match include fresh tomatoes and asparagus, fresh citrus fruits, and spicy condiments. If any of these items dominates, it may be best to serve a high acid sparkling wine as a palate cleanser or plain water. In such cases where they are lightly included, choose a simple, uncomplicated wine that is not too fruity or packed with too many flavors: Chenin Blancs, table whites, or wines that refresh without distracting from the food.

Wines often do not go well with salads dressed with vinaigrette. Use a cream or cheese dressing. Wines can seem dull with fresh, crisp greens. Within a course or even among several courses, there is usually a logical progression of flavors and the wines should be considered. As wine warms, it develops and changes flavors. If several wines and courses are served, they should progress together: lighter wines and dishes before heavier ones. Fruit and nutty flavors often offer interesting contrasts.

In any event, wine in moderation can have healthful benefits. Also, moderate amounts of wine enhance not only the food but the joy of the evening and the well-being of the diners.

A very simple explanation of wine is that grapes ferment naturally to make wine. During the process, yeasts help convert the grape sugar to alcohol and carbonic acid gas (which escapes). The fermentation can be stopped before all the sugar is converted. Such wines have residual sugar and varying degrees of sweetness. When the sugar is totally converted, the wines are dry.

White wines can be sweet or dry, light or medium to full-bodied. The sweeter products (usually Chenin Blancs, Rieslings, Colombards, blush wines, some Gewurztraminers and proprietary wines) go with Mexican foods and other highly seasoned foods. The dryer products go especially well with seafoods, fowl, rabbit and veal (usually Sauvignon Blanc and Chardonnay), but sauces and seasonings make a difference. Red wines are generally more full-bodied and dry and go well with beef, lamb, and game (Cabernet Sauvignon, Pinot Noir, Zinfandel, Merlot). Fall Creek Carnelian and Sanchez Creek Chambourcin are dry, medium-bodied red wines. Sparkling wines are suitable for most dishes and occasions. The good acidity in dry sparkling wine helps clean the palate.

3.

Vintages

Vintages are tremendously important to wine. Most winemakers agree that wine is made in the vineyard, meaning, the vicissitudes of weather help determine the health and quality of the grape which makes the wine.

The decade of the 1980s was extraordinary. At one point, it seemed the vintages were playing one-upmanship to see which could better the other. Certainly 1985, 1986, and 1987 fit this description. That's not to exclude the others. In 1989 I had a Clos du Bois 1981 Briarcrest, Buena Vista 1982 Cabernet Sauvignon, Beringer Knights Valley 1983 Cabernet Sauvignon, and 1984 Shafer and a Cain Cellars Cabernet Sauvignon — and all were beautiful wines. Of course, weather is not equal in all areas. The rain does not fall nor the sun shine evenly on every plot of vineyard. Not all vineyards can be picked at precisely the same time. Various lots of grapes will differ. That, among other things, accounts for some bottles being better than others. But nature, viticulture, and technology have combined with human art to create some amazing vintages.

Most wine drinkers don't want a precise, season-by-season weather report of each appellation. Such information could well fill a volume all its own. Vintage information often focuses on red varietals, since overall the red wines age for longer periods of time than white ones. White wines, generally — but of course with exceptions — are made to be drunk young, within two years of the vintage. Weather certainly gives an indication of expectation in both red and white wines, but it is only one measure, albeit, a very major one. The following general vintage notes should be useful.

*VINTAGE NOTES**

The spring and summer of 1974 were cool and the vines produced only a moderate crop. As harvest approached the growers and winemakers became apprehensive about the predicted rains. However, the valley basked in sunshine and warm days in late September and October, providing excellent grape quality. The 1974 grapes were excellent in both sugar and acid and earned the reputation as the great vintage from Napa Valley.

In 1978, a good winter rainfall ended the drought and produced a fine growing year which was shortened by a very warm harvest. Ample spring rains followed by a warm summer matured the Cabernet Sauvignon grapes with an excellent balance of sugar and acid. It produced full-bodied wines well balanced with fruit.

The 1980 vintage has been acclaimed by experts as outstanding. A cool summer followed by a hot September brought the late ripening Cabernet grapes to a balance of both high acid and sugar — an ideal combination for producing wines of superior quality.

The 1981 harvest was the earliest since 1941. It began with an early, mild spring and was followed by a warm, dry summer. The usual cooling fogs of July and August were few, thus the Cabernet grapes moved rapidly to maturity and were harvested about ten days ahead of normal. The fruit was rich with good varietal intensity and a well-balanced sugar/acid ratio.

The 1982 Napa Valley growing season was a challenging one and long will be remembered for a record rainfall. The vintage began with heavy spring rain, causing the bud-break to occur about two weeks late. The growing season throughout the summer was cool, and the grapes enjoyed the usual early morning fog. This cool weather delayed the harvest but allowed the grapes to mature slowly and evenly.

---

* (Courtesy, for the most part, of Inglenook, Napa Valley)

Curious weather and a small crop were products of 1983. Many vines had a normal pattern of maturation, despite the coast being unusually warm and the usually hot Central Valley unseasonably cool. A wet winter, heavy abnormal rainfall, and Indian summer generally made the 1983 vintage a difficult year for wine grapes. In the Napa Valley, the 1983 growing season led to a vintage of high quality but lower quantity than in previous years. The season began normally with bud-break occurring around April 1. Temperatures throughout the summer were fairly cool except for a mid-July heat wave. By the end of August, two days of light rain had caused little concern as the warm weather quickly returned in the first two weeks of September. This period of warmth allowed the Cabernet Sauvignon to reach maturity, and the harvested grapes were in excellent condition.

Early, heavy rainfalls in November/December 1983 were followed by below average spring rains in 1984. Higher than normal temperatures started vine growth early, and veraison (grapes change color just before harvest) came on fast in all varieties. The fruit was early but clean and in good condition. Napa recorded thirty-four days over 100 degrees F. and thirteen days between 105 and 108 degrees. There was a heat wave in September — 90 degrees or more daily (ten degrees above normal). Some grapes had higher sugar than desired. The 1984 vintage was earliest in history. Excellent vintage for Cabernet — considered the best since 1978.

The 1985 vintage was preceded by adequate winter rainfall and began with an early bud-break. A cool spring was followed by fluctuating temperatures in June, a condition which increased berry shatter or shot berry (terms for *coulure* or *millerandage* — uneven berry development which leads to a small crop), and decreased the yield per acre. Although July was warm, the remainder of the season had relatively cool temperatures and maintained a high acidity in grapes. This well-balanced composition in the grapes produced wines with excellent structure. Often called the "vintage of the decade," 1985 provided the optimum balance of early-season warmth with a cool, extended maturation period. This exceptional vintage allowed the grapes to develop enhanced varietal character and impeccable balance.

There was a long, cool growing season in 1986 which allowed the fruit to develop slowly and evenly. Heavy rains occurred mid-harvest for some varieties. Temperatures were slightly erratic, but the Cabernet Sauvignon displays lovely color and has great flavor: excellent Chardonnays also. Definitely a vintage to watch.

The year 1987 brought an outstanding vintage. The early growing season was characterized by warm, occasionally hot temperatures. The classic, cooling fog extended the growing season, protecting the acidity of the fruit and allowing the grapes to ripen slowly and fully. Low rainfall limited the growth of the vines and the resulting smaller berries and clusters exhibited intense varietal flavors.

Sonoma County is adjacent to Napa. The counties are similar but not identical, just as microclimates within each county vary considerably. The counties are separated by mountains that also affect the climates somewhat differently. Both Napa and Sonoma have maritime climates and both get additional heat in the northern regions and cooler climate in the southern regions. Still, I've included some vintage notes for comparative purposes. (Courtesy Château Souverain, Geyserville, Sonoma County.)

Sonoma County, 1985, had a long, cool growing season that resulted in one of the finest vintages in history for red wines. A long season allowed for a steady, gradual ripening of the grapes. The even-paced vintage provided Cabernet fruit with excellent acidity, deep color and firm tannins, all well balanced. The weather at harvest mirrored that of the summer; ideal conditions for Cabernet to reach full maturity. Harvesting started September 16 and was completed October 14.

In 1987, buds broke on the vines earlier than usual due to a dry winter and early spring warmth. Vine growth was accelerated by an exceptionally warm spell in May. Temperatures were moderate through summer but soared back up in August. Growing temperatures resulted in perfectly ripened grapes.

*WINE FACTS**

A. Worldwide Wine Production averages 1981–1987, percentages of total

1. Italy: 1,937 million gallons, 22%
2. France: 1,811 million gallons, 21%

---

* (Courtesy Wine Institute, 164 Post Street, San Francisco, CA 94108)

3. Spain: 921 million gallons, 15.5%
4. U.S.S.R.: 866 million gallons, 10%
5. U.S.A.: 476 million gallons, 5.5%
6. California: 428 million gallons, 5%
7. Other countries: 2,715 million gallons, 31%
8. All countries: 8,726 million gallons, 100%

B. U.S.A. Wine Production
1. California: 428 million gallons, 91%
2. New York: 27 million gallons, 6%
3. Washington: 5 million gallons, 1%
4. Other states: 13 million gallons, 3%

C. Per Capita Consumption, five-year trend
1. Italy: 20.87 gallons, -14%
2. France: 19.84, -12%
3. U.S.A.: 2.25 gallons, -6%
4. California: 4.17%, -8%

There are 324,000 acres of varietal wine grapes in California, including 42,000 acres of Chardonnay, 30,000 acres of Zinfandel, and 26,000 acres of Cabernet Sauvignon.

In Texas there are approximately twenty-five wineries and the estimate of grape acreage as of March 1988 was 4,650 acres. Most of the small wine production is consumed within the state, but demand is increasing the production and the potential for broader markets looks good.

Wine, of course, is a living commodity. It changes daily. After it is opened it changes minute by minute. A wine tasted at the beginning of the meal seldom smells or tastes the same an hour or more later.

In general, white wines should be drunk within two years of the vintage date on the bottle. Those who prefer light, fresh fruity white wines should drink the most recent vintage. White wines which are barrel fermented are more full-bodied and will age in the bottle, generally five years or so. There are, of course, exceptions, but for the purposes of using this book, the suggestions apply.

Red wines are more complex because the grapes ferment on their skins. The extracts from the skin contribute more characteristics to the wine. Tannins from the grape skins and barrels help red wines to age. The greater the time the wine spends in contact with these and other substances, the bigger the wine and the longer it ages. Weather affects the grape skin structure. At the right time, sun strengthens it, and at the wrong time, rain weakens it. Thicker skins generally have more tannin. Some red wines age well for twenty, forty, or more years; however, Americans seem to prefer younger wines. Most California and Texas fine red wines are aged three, four, or more years before they are released. Consequently, most of them are ready to drink when released to the public. Even so, many of them will age well for several years more in a proper cellar; generally seven to ten years is about average.

It is exciting to explore the world of wines. There are so many interesting types to discover and enjoy in moderation. Judge the wines for yourself and trust your own palate.

Just like food items on a menu, wines on a wine list also change. Some of the wines listed here (most on restaurant wine lists) will still be available and some will not. Even so, they should be available at wine and spirits shops or in supermarkets for your enjoyment at home.

4.

Proprietary Wines

One category of wines, proprietary wines, I think deserves special attention. As a "genre," for they are truly works of art, they comprise some of the best products the American wine industry is releasing. Although not binding, a new name for this group, Meritage, was selected by an association composed of many of the principals who produce these wines. Discussion among wine enthusiasts has been varied about the name.

In any event, contrary to Shakespeare's notion that a rose "by any other name would smell as sweet," winemakers are discovering that a wine by another name may smell and taste better.

Naming wines has an interesting history. Since Roman times, and even earlier, wines have been given geographical names for their place of origin, whether it was a district (Burgundy) or perhaps a river (Rhine). Many Europeans who came to America and made wine continued to use the familiar French, German, and other names for their wines. Over the years laws changed the practice somewhat and other preferences also have influenced naming wines.

In his book *The Wines of America,* Leon Adams recorded a trend established by journalist/importer Frank Schoonmaker. In 1939 he gathered an assortment of the best American wines he had discovered, had them bottled at wineries under his "Schoonmaker's Selections," and offered them to the public. He refused to call American wines by European place names and decided to call them by the principal grape variety in the wine. It was not a new notion, but he added unknown names to the list: Pinot Blanc, Chardonnay, Semillon, Pinot Noir, and others. His excellent selections with the exotic names meant a rare quality to connoisseurs who began to include them in previously all-European wine collections.

Other vintners adopted the idea, and varietal wines became synonymous with the best. Eventually, law dictated that bottles with varietal labels must contain at least seventy-five percent of that grape. Frequently, the beverage was and is made from 100 percent of the grape named on the bottle, and many fine wines are represented. In the 1970s, however, several American vintners recognized that some of the finest European wines were blends, not limited by permitted amounts of varietals. They wanted to create wines as fine as the European models. The answer in many instances has been proprietary wines which do not include the varietal name on the bottle. They are named ostensibly by the property owner with such fetching terms as L'Annee, Insignia, Dominus, Opus One, Trilogy, and Sterling Vineyards Three Palms.

Today the trendy proprietary wines are capturing the coveted definitions of best and rare, and often, most expensive. They are not new to the wine industry. Fanciful names often are given to blended wines of varying quality and cost. Not so, however, with the products which began in 1974 at the Joseph Phelps Winery. These and other proprietary wines select the best grapes from the best lots of the best vineyards. Everything about them is special, from the name to the finished product.

L'Annee, for example, was created to celebrate the 130th anniversary of Buena Vista Winery and Vineyards. According to President Marcus Moller-Racke, it is a super-premium proprietary red wine, the first release containing 51.4 percent Cabernet Sauvignon and 48.6 percent Merlot.

"The name for this wine," he says, "had to signify something important, not only our heritage and tradition but also what we've been working so hard to accomplish since we purchased Buena Vista in 1979. We chose the French word for 'year' because we felt our 130th anniversary was truly the year for Buena Vista."

At Joseph Phelps Vineyards, the proprietary wine is Insignia.

It claims the pacesetter position as the first (1974) such luxury blend wine introduced. Winemaker Craig Williams sees Insignia as a provocative challenge. He believes there are important differences in how grape flavors and aromas are extracted and that there is an ongoing experimentation in how grapes are turned into wine.

"There are many layers in blending wine and they change yearly by varying the amounts of Cabernet Sauvignon, Merlot and Cabernet Franc," he says. "Insignia has given me a greater appreciation for appellations in Napa. There are differences in how and where grapes are grown. Now, rather than analytical chemistry, I rely on observation and personal experience. That's what it's all about. It's farming."

Other wineries offer fine wines which also vary the blend. Winemaker John Hawley believes the Clos du Bois Marlstone, from Marlstone Vineyard, maximizes quality and consistently produces a complex and balanced wine by varying the proportions of the components. Marlstone was first released in 1978.

"Merlot softens the tannins in the Cabernet Sauvignon; Cabernet Franc adds spice and complexity, while the small amount of Malbec gives the wine added color and body," Hawley says. "This wine has consistently won awards since being released and its high quality makes it a benchmark for California wines of this style."

The luxury wine named Opus One is a joint venture between the families of Robert Mondavi and Baron Philippe de Rothschild. Robert Mondavi and the baron began discussing the possibility in the early 1970s.

"He called on me twice," Mondavi says. "There was nothing definite then, but he wanted a Cabernet Sauvignon and we couldn't decide exactly what we wanted to do. In 1978 I was a guest at the Château where we shared 100-year-old Mouton. The baron did 90% of his business in his bedroom, dressed in a silk dressing robe and with his retriever settled at his feet. We discussed the quantity, winery and vineyards, the name, percentages, number of wines, and decided on 5,000 cases of only one wine. We got 140 acres in the heart of the best land in Napa. We profit from each other, our research and the French tradition of winemaking."

Another joint venture is Dominus. The wine is the product of Christian Moueix of Château Petrus fame in Pomerol and the John Daniel Society. Grapes are from the Napanook Vineyard, and co-owner Robin Lail explained the pursuit.

"Dominus was a lifelong dream of mine," she says. "My father owned Inglenook Winery and my sister [Marcia Smith] and I inherited Napanook Vineyard. I was working for Bob Mondavi, a fantastic mentor, when Moueix contacted him in 1981 about a venture project. Mondavi put us together in December and everything clicked. We formed the John Daniel Society in May 1982. Our philosophy is so simple — to produce one of the great red wines of the world."

In May 1988, Geyser Peak released the Vintage 1984 Reserve Alexandre. It was a blend of four grapes, one more (Malbec) than the first offering in 1983. Future bottles will contain Petit Verdot, which is also grown by Geyser Peak. The vineyards are in Alexander Valley, hence the name, and the label shows an ancient silver coin with the profile of Alexander the Great as well as the percentages of the component grapes. CEO John McClelland explained that California winemakers are just beginning to grow all the varieties of Bordeaux grapes used to make proprietary wines.

"We use the other grapes in combination with the Cabernet Sauvignon because most unblended California Cabernets have not indicated a longevity as great as the First Growths of Bordeaux," he says. "Reserve Alexandre was designed to last twenty-five years or more."

At Flora Springs the magic word is Trilogy. It was five years in the making and so named because the first release (1984) happened to be equal portions of the three grapes used: Cabernet Sauvignon, Merlot, and Cabernet Franc. Members of the Komes and Garvey families own and manage the property where grapes are grown in five Napa Valley locations, kept in separate lots and blended for aging in barrel.

"All grapes come from our 400 acres," Julie Komes Garvey says. "We sell eighty percent of them. The purpose of Trilogy is to make the best possible wine from our grapes. My husband Pat manages the vineyard and he says we don't try to improve a style on the fruit but try to bring it to its highest potential. It's a severe selection process. This isn't the biggest wine we could make but it is the most complete. We believe blends are the wave of the future."

Together with the tremendous overhauling and upgrading experienced at Christian Brothers over the past several years is the introduction of a new product named Montage. There are two wines, a red and a white, which are blends from France and California.

According to Ron Batori, vice-president/public relations, the idea had been percolating through the mind of Dick Maher, president of Christian Brothers, for some years.

"The reason for Montage is to blend to the best taste we can achieve," Batori says. "The French red wine is from the Haut Medoc and the white comes from the Macon region. The 1985 red wine is sixty percent French and forty percent Californian from the Oakville Ranch. The 1985 white is sixty-five percent Californian Chardonnay and thirty-five percent French. Montage is not intended to make either of the two components better but to have a unique wine that's slightly more interesting than either one alone. California brings fruit on the nose, forwardness and power, while the French component brings structure and length."

There are other worthy proprietary wines. Lyeth is certainly among them. From its beginning, Lyeth Vineyard and Winery has produced only two wines, a Bordeaux-style red and a white. Each one uses a blend of traditional Bordeaux grapes: Cabernet Sauvignon, Merlot, Cabernet Franc, and Malbec for the Lyeth red table wine; Sauvignon Blanc, Semillon, and Muscadelle du Bordelais for the Lyeth white table wine. Other than the name Lyeth, the vintage, and the Alexander Valley appellation, there is no additional designation on the handsome, classic label. Both wines were listed under the highest category (★★★★★ Outstanding Producers) by wine authority Robert Parker in his book *Wine Buyer's Guide*. They are lovely, elegant, soft yet intensely flavored wines.

The big news at Cain Cellars is the release of their first estate-grown claret. In May 1989, wine lovers were treated to their prestigious Cain Five, an incomparably rich and sumptuous proprietor's blend of Cabernet Sauvignon, Cabernet Franc, Malbec, Merlot, and Petit Verdot — the quintessence of a Bordeaux-style wine. Winemaker Lester Hardy is duly proud.

"In blending we look especially for a silky texture and an agreeable mouth feel," he says. "The wine will have some tannin, as any good red wine will, but we choose a blend without coarseness or harshness and we emphasize length and continuity of flavor. The complexity and richness merge naturally as a consequence of the multi-varietal blending."

Only 2,500 cases are available.

Making its debut in 1983, Merryvale is another producer with a strikingly handsome label showing the embossed profiles of the owners across the top. This luscious wine combines Cabernet Sauvignon, Merlot, and Cabernet Franc and is made at Merryvale's wholly owned subsidiary, Sunny St. Helena Winery — the first winemaking facility built in Napa Valley after Prohibition. It has been completely restored. The Merryvale red table wine is definitely worth discovering. President Robin Lail (also a partner in Dominus) and I tasted the 1983, 1984, and 1985 vintages which showed a consistent style, delicate and elegant with plenty of fruit and firm structure.

George Vierra, a former winemaker at Robert Mondavi, founded Vichon Winery in 1980, now owned by Mondavi. Vierra's latest creation is Merlion Winery, founded in 1985. The name, he explained, is the medieval title for both a small falcon and Merlin, the legendary Arthurian magician.

"We intend the character of our wines and winemaking to reflect the fascinating flight of this elegant bird and the ingenuity and magical delights of the magician," he says. "Our winemaker, John McKay, has been making fine Napa Valley wines for over fifteen years. Merlion wines are designed to illustrate the 'complementary' style of winemaking, that is, producing a fine, naturally balanced wine which pairs harmoniously with fine foods."

The Merlion Sauvier is fifty percent Sauvignon Blanc and fifty percent Semillon, a proprietary blend Vierra believes embodies the best qualities of these two varietals. It's a pale yellow wine with hints of herbs and fruit, a tart, clean, wine with a nice finish.

Two recent additions to the proprietary category are Homage from Clos Pegase (1988) and Antares from Hacienda (1989).

Homage is a blend of primarily Cabernet Franc and Merlot with small amounts of Cabernet Sauvignon and Petite Sirah for added complexity. Antares is a red blend of sixty-five percent Cabernet Sauvignon, twenty percent Cabernet Franc, and fifteen percent Merlot. (Antares is the name of the brightest star in the southern sky.) Both wines have found their niche.

Another chapter has been recorded concerning these Bordeaux-style blended wines. A group of proprietary producers formed an organization with the purpose of finding a distinctive name for their wines. Early in 1989, after sorting through 6,000 entries that responded to the contest, they selected Meritage. The response has been mixed and only time will tell how widespread usage becomes.

Current members of the Meritage Association include Bellerose, Beringer, Carmenet, Clos du Bois, Concannonn, Cosentino, de Lorimier, Dominus, Dry Creek, Flora Springs, Franciscan, Geyser Peak, Glen Ellen, The Hess Collection, Iron Horse, Jekel, Robert Keenan, Konocti, Lyeth, Merlion, Meridian, Merryvale, Murphy-Goode, Pahlmeyer, Joseph Phelps, Pine Ridge, Rombauer, Sterling, Vichon, Woodward, Canyon and Zaca Mesa.

To use the Meritage certification mark a winery must comply with standards established by the Meritage Association. The wine must be blended entirely (100 percent) from Bordeaux grape varieties and it must be the winery's top-of-the-line wine. It won't be designated a varietal wine although the varieties may be listed with their percentages on the label. Also, the wine must be produced and bottled by the winery located in the U.S. and carry its appellation of origin. Production is limited to 25,000 cases per vintage.

The wines indicate top quality, luscious, rich wines, with layers of interesting flavors, aromas, and complexity.

OPUS ONE: An Example

When the families of the Robert Mondavi-Rothschild (RMR) joint venture wine, Opus One, broke ground for the winery, they celebrated the event with a "Fete Champetre," a festival in the countryside among the vineyards at the site of the future building.

In addition, Opus One winemakers Tim Mondavi and Patrick Leon gave a vertical tasting of all vintages to date, 1979 to 1986. It was extraordinary to taste all those wines, each with superlative flavors, each beautifully integrated and structured, varying in excellence only as a result of weather. It was a one-time experience, unlikely to be repeated, so I recorded my tasting notes for this book.

1979 Opus One — Eighty percent Cabernet Sauvignon, sixteen percent Cabernet Franc, four percent Merlot.

Color: Brick red with mahogany tinges.

Aroma/bouquet: A forward, rich nose with layers of fruit odors.

Taste: Complex meld of flavors; rich with spice, berries and hints of oak; unresolved tannins add firmness without harshness; well-balanced and smooth; ready to drink but will keep a bit longer.

1980 Opus One — Ninety-six percent Cabernet Sauvignon, four percent Cabernet Franc.

Color: Brick with magenta.

Aroma/bouquet: Nose more closed and less fragrant; tighter structure of odors.

Taste: Some olive, tar, spice, and cinnamon; a big wine with a centralized structure; concentrated and a well-knit texture.

1981 Opus One — Ninety-three percent Cabernet Sauvignon, seven percent Cabernet Franc.

Color: Garnet/cranberry with a tinge of brick.

Aroma/bouquet: Myriad odors of fruits, spice, and oak.

Taste: A well-integrated, rich, and plummy wine; mellow and velvety; nice acidity with elegance and finesse.

1982 Opus One — Eighty percent Cabernet Sauvignon, sixteen percent Cabernet Franc, four percent Merlot.

Color: Deep blood red with royal blue/red tinges.

Aroma/bouquet: Integrated nose with series of fruit and mild spice.

Taste: Nice and perfumy; fruitiness; substantial tannins with ripe flavors and oak; big wine, mouth filling; lingers; aging power.

1983 Opus One — Eighty percent Cabernet Sauvignon, fourteen percent Cabernet Franc, seven percent Merlot.

Color: Bright ruby red.

Aroma/bouquet: Layers of plum, berries, jam, and spice.

Taste: Chewy tannins; lovely fruit; marvelous complexity; vanillins and ripe plums, berries and spices; elegant and nice finish.

1984 Opus One — Ninety-seven percent Cabernet Sauvignon, seven percent Cabernet Franc.

Color: Deep dark pidgeon blood ruby.

Aroma/bouquet: Cranberry and spice, complex bouquet of various delicious aromas; floral fragrances.

Taste: Fruitiness with well-structured tannins but with softness on palate; lovely mixed flavors and spices; elegant and finishes nicely.

1985 Opus One — Ninety percent Cabernet Sauvignon, four percent Cabernet Franc, six percent Merlot.

Color: Ruby with purple tinges.

Aroma/bouquet: Freshness, ripe fruit medley, rich raisins, and sweet fruit.

Taste: Silky on palate; lovely texture; unresolved tannins add structure; nicely balanced with fruit; firm and lingering flavors of fruit and spice, marvelous wine.

1986 Opus One — Eighty-seven percent Cabernet Sauvignon, nine percent Cabernet Franc, four percent Merlot.

Color: Rich, royal purple red.

Aroma/bouquet: Rich medley of fruitiness — cassis, blueberries, and spices.

Taste: Fruits and young chewy tannins; nice complexity; big tannins but beautifully balanced with fruit and multiple underlying flavors; lovely wine.

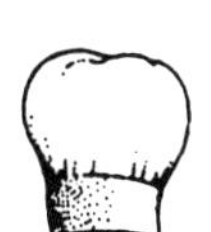

Part III

Menus & Chefs

About the Chefs

Thomson, Rausch, Pyles, Prambs, Platz, O'Leary, Molzan, McGrath, Mannke, Keating, Holben and Holben, Greer, Gielisse, Fearing, Del Grande, Burklé, Brandt, Blank, and Auden — the mere mention of these chefs' names fills the head with mesmerizing aromas, visions of delectable morsels, and a litany of praises. The creations of each chef are unique, more than just delicious food arranged attractively on a plate. Their preparations reflect values, attitudes, and personality. Consequently, I wanted a markedly entertaining way to present their biographies, something different that would show their individuality. I decided on twenty-six questions that they could answer in their own style. Some answered a portion of them and some answered all; some answered at length and some answered with brevity; some answered seriously and some with levity, but in each instance, the format remained true in revealing distinctive characteristics of that particular chef.

Generally, about half of the top chefs like chocolate cake, more than a fourth play musical instruments, several have gardens, most of them have never been to a fortune teller, and almost all chefs work seventy hours or more a week.

Presentation of the Q/A form posed somewhat of a problem; that is, how to avoid tiring the reader with repetitious questions. The narrative approach was the answer, and, inadvertently, Paul Bocuse and Brillat-Savarin helped with their use of aphorisms. Using their style gives the book a sense of continuity as well as quotable thoughts.

The questions asked the chefs follow.

Name, birthday and place of birth:

What did you want to be named?

What's your favorite birthday cake?

Name your favorite celebration:

Culinary training:

What have fortune tellers told you?

Awards and recognitions:

Most esteemed honor:

Shoes worn in the kitchen:

Hours per week in kitchen:

Favorite dish to cook:

Favorite dish to eat:

Worst disaster you've ever prepared:

Most embarrassing culinary moment:

Best culinary moment:

Most fun event:

Most difficult preparation:

How do you spend your day off?

What's your favorite tip to cooks?

Name the best shortcut:

What's the most successful substitute?

Your philosophy?

Your definition of junk food. Do you eat it?

Preferred restaurants for your personal dining:
Reasons for preference:

Do you sing or whistle while you cook? Opera, jazz, popular, western or what?

Bruce James Auden

Born March 7, 1955, in London, England, Bruce Auden wanted to be called Jay or James as a child, but says he likes Bruce just fine now. His favorite birthday cake, as a child and an adult, has always been his mom's chocolate cake: "She uses good English chocolate and always bakes it for me."

His favorite tip to cooks is to use the freezer. "I use mine for garlic in oil, fresh herbs puréed into a paste and put in oil and for ginger root, but not the frozen meats most people use it for."

The sensitive and romantic Chef Auden's favorite celebration is his wedding anniversary.

As a converted Texan, he was especially pleased to be named "Who's Who in Food and Wine in Texas," and thinks his most fun event is the Texas Hill Country Wine and Food Festival.

Auden used to find pasta difficult to prepare but thinks he has gotten better at making it. He prefers to cook any kind of game — squab, duck, venison. However, his favorite dish to eat is salads, which may explain his extremely slender physique — 6′1 and 135 pounds.

"Junk food to me is pastries like Twinkies and stadium food — nachos and such, anything with a lot of fat and sodium — and no, I don't eat it," he says.

He spends his day off in the garden or riding his bike with his wife in the Texas Hill Country.

Aphorisms of Bruce Auden

1. Don't look at recipes as if they were the gospel. Experiment.
2. The best culinary moment is when you work on an item you've been thinking about and it all comes together.
3. It's an honor when people are enthusiastic about your food.
4. If you spend more than ten to twelve hours a day in the kitchen, it's too much.
5. Don't substitute canned goods for fresh and always use the best ingredients you can.
6. Experience helps you handle situations in the kitchen better, so disasters are less disastrous.

CHEF BRUCE AUDEN

Auden's Restaurant
San Antonio
(to open in the future)

Menu

Chipotle Spiced Steak Tartare on Malanga
Fall Creek Carnelian, Hacienda Pinot Noir, or
J. Lohr Chenin Blanc

Bacon, Lettuce, and Tomato Soup
Llano Estacado Chenin Blanc or J. Lohr Johannisberg Riesling

Roasted Chicken Salad with Orange on Arugula
Christian Brothers Barrel Fermented Chardonnay or
Fall Creek Sauvignon Blanc

Aromatic Medallions of Lamb on Plantains
with Tamarind Spiced Peanuts
Kenwood Sauvignon Blanc, Gundlach-Bundschu Pinot Noir, or
Clos du Val Merlot

Gingered Rice Pudding on Persimmon Purée
with Dried Tart Cherry Conserve
Coffee
Grand Cru Late Harvest Gewurztraminer or
Mirassou Sparkling Brut

CHIPOTLE SPICED STEAK TARTARE ON MALANGA

As any steak tartare is a question of individual taste, I suggest that each ingredient be added in small amounts to assure the final taste is as you want it to be.

Yield: about 16 patties (depending on size)

1 lb. chopped lean steak
1/4 can of chipotle peppers in adobo sauce, chopped fine
2 tbsp. onions, chopped fine (1015s, if possible)
1 tbsp. cilantro, lightly chopped
1 tbsp. parsley, lightly chopped
1/4 cup queso caribe, small dice (a Mexican cheese similar to a farmer's cheese; Auden likes it because it doesn't melt completely)
1 egg yolk
1 medium tomato, small dice
1 tsp. lime juice
1/2 tsp. annato powder for color (available in Latin or Oriental markets)
Pinch kosher salt

When you have combined these ingredients to your taste, lightly pat into rounds and place on a nest made of wisps of fried malanga root (a tuber like a yam, found in specialty food stores). Garnish with mustard greens or kale and diced tomatoes and cheese.

BACON, LETTUCE, AND TOMATO SOUP

Serves 6–8

8 slices of bacon
2 cloves garlic, crushed
1/2 white onion, julienned
1 1/2 qts. chicken broth
1 qt. heavy whipping cream
1 small bunch of fresh thyme
10 peppercorns
8 slices of trimmed white bread

Garnish:

2 big tomatoes, seeded and diced
1/2 head romaine lettuce, julienned
1 cup croutons

Cook bacon until crisp; save fat. In a large pot sauté garlic and onion in bacon fat. Add chicken broth and reduce 1/3. Add cream, thyme, and peppercorns and bring to a boil. Add salt and pepper to taste. Strain; add bread and blend in for 30 seconds. Add garnishes.

Note: Keep tomatoes warm when adding to the soup or soup will lose heat.

ROASTED CHICKEN SALAD WITH ORANGE ON ARUGULA

Serves 8

2 large garlic cloves, mashed
1/4 cup orange juice
1/4 cup chicken stock
2 tsp. rosemary, fresh and chopped
2 tsp. oregano, fresh and chopped
2 tsp. orange zest
1 tbsp. chopped onion
1/4 tsp. kosher salt
1 serrano pepper, fresh and chopped
1/4 cup cider vinegar
2 chicken breasts on the bone
Orange sections, cucumbers, tomatoes, celery, onions, peppers, zucchini, etc., and arugula or other bitter greens
3/4 cup olive oil

In a blender combine first ten ingredients and blend until smooth. Cover chicken with this mixture and marinate 45 minutes. Using any combination of vegetables, herbs, greens, and such, make a bed on a platter or individual plates.

Remove the chicken from the marinade and roast in a 400-degree oven for 30 minutes. Meanwhile, reduce marinade over medium heat until reduced by 1/2. Cool to room temperature and mix in olive oil; check seasonings.

When chicken is ready, shred into strips and place over salad. Pour dressing over. Nuts, cheese, or more herbs can be added, if desired.

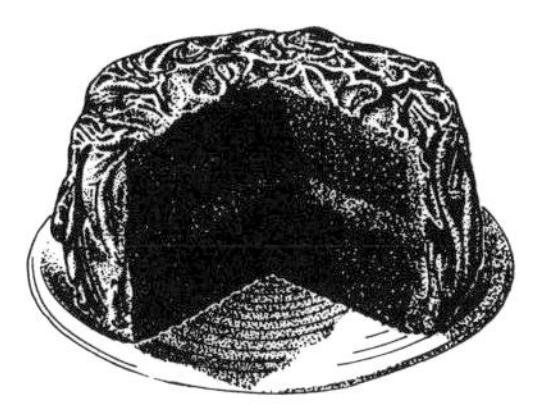

AROMATIC MEDALLIONS OF LAMB ON PLANTAINS WITH TAMARIND SPICED PEANUTS

Serves 4

1 plantain, ripe
1 cup peanut oil
1 lb. loin of lamb
1½-inch piece of ginger
1 cup plain yogurt
3 cloves of garlic, lightly crushed
2-inch stick of cinnamon
6 cardamom pods
10 whole cloves
5 De Arbol chili peppers (dried)
Pinch of ground cumin
½ cup of tamarind spiced peanuts (recipe follows)
Mint and cilantro leaves

Peel and slice the plantain into ¼-inch slices at an angle. Heat ½ of the oil in a pan and fry plantain until brown, turning once. Remove and dry on paper towels.

Slice lamb into medallions. Peel and grate the ginger and mix with ½ of the yogurt. Marinate lamb in yogurt and ginger for three hours.

Heat the rest of the oil until hot but not smoking. Add garlic and stir for 20 seconds, then add cinnamon, cardamom, cloves, and De Arbol chilies. Stir for 20 seconds until flavors have infused into oil. Wipe marinade off the lamb and sauté the lamb in flavored oil until medium rare.

Mix the rest of the yogurt with the cumin. Place the lamb on plantain, top with a little cumin yogurt and peanut mix and mint or cilantro leaf.

Tamarind peanuts with coconut

1 cup raw peanuts
¼ cup fresh grated coconut
2 tbsp. tamarind paste dissolved in 4 tbsp. boiling water
2 tbsp. sugar
1 tsp. peanut oil
Pinch of salt

Toss ingredients together and roast at 350 degrees. Turn and stir mixture often until peanuts are coated and crisp and dark glazed.

GINGERED RICE PUDDING ON PERSIMMON PURÉE WITH DRIED TART CHERRY CONSERVE

Serves 8

1 qt. half-and-half
2 pts. heavy cream
1 cup rice
1 cup sugar
2-inch piece of fresh ginger, sliced but still in one piece
1/2 vanilla bean, split
Pinch kosher salt
5 egg yolks
1 pt. heavy cream, whipped firm
1 pt. persimmon purée (recipe follows)
1 cup cranberry-cactus pear sauce (recipe follows)
1 cup maple chocolate sauce (recipe follows)
1 pt. tart cherry conserve (recipe follows)

Combine first seven ingredients in a heavy-bottomed pan. Bring to a boil and simmer for at least one hour or until mixture becomes thick. Stir often, using a wooden spoon to prevent sticking. When mixture is thick remove from heat. Take out ginger and vanilla bean and stir in yolks well while mixture is hot. Cool mixture in refrigerator, stirring occasionally. When completely cool, fold in firm whipped cream (the amount of cream added will depend on how thick the pudding will be). If the pudding is not firm enough to serve on a plate, spoon into cups and glaze under your broiler until brown and serve in the cup.

To arrange plate presentation, cover plate with 2 oz. of persimmon purée. Highlight with drizzles of cranberry sauce. Spoon on rice pudding and drizzle with chocolate sauce. Spoon conserve onto plate and garnish with mint.

Persimmon purée

3 large, overripe persimmons
Apple juice or other juice as needed

Squeeze pulp of persimmons out of their skins into blender and purée. Thin to right consistency with juice and strain.

Cranberry-cactus pear sauce

1 cup cranberries
4 cactus pear (red) pulp
Juice of 3 oranges
Zest of 1 orange

Combine all ingredients and bring to a boil. Simmer for 10 minutes; remove from heat. Remove zest and purée in blender. Strain and cool.

Note: Sauce will be very tart. If you are using for another dish, it should be sweetened.

Maple chocolate sauce

3 oz. bittersweet chocolate in small pieces
1 oz. maple syrup

Combine over a double boiler, stirring until chocolate is completely melted. Keep warm until ready to use.

Dried tart cherry conserve

2 cups dried cherries★
2 cups apple cider
2 tsp. lemon juice
1 cup sugar
Pinch ground cinnamon (to taste)
Pinch ground cloves (to taste)
1/2 cup pecan halves

Combine first 3 ingredients; cover and cook about 10 minutes until cherries are soft. Remove cover and add rest of ingredients except nuts. Slowly bring to a boil, stirring occasionally. Boil for about 10 minutes, stirring often. Add nuts the last 3 minutes of cooking. Remove and serve at room temperature.

★ Available from: American Spoon Foods
411 E. Lake St.
Petoskey, Michigan 49880
(616) 347-9030
(800) 222-5886

Jeffrey Harrison Blank

Born June 29, 1950, in Pittsburg, Pennsylvania, Jeffrey Blank liked his name but considered spelling it Geoffrey, like his British great-great-great-grandfather's name.

Contrary to his British heritage, his favorite celebration is American. "I love Thanksgiving because it is a celebration of family, country, and food and the beginning of the holiday season," he says.

Much to his surprise, a fortune teller revealed that Blank had been a chef in a previous life.

He has been featured on the cover of *M* magazine, in a feature article in the *New York Times,* in the PBS series "Chefs of the West," on the BBC Keith Floyd series "Floyd's American Pie," and was nominated to the "Tribute to James Beard Meals on Wheels" in New York City.

When asked about his favorite dish to cook, he replied, "I can't isolate one dish, but I enjoy preparing sauces and cooking the sauté station. They allow more personal touches and finesse. For eating, I love seafood and pasta with lobster, shrimp, scallops, crab, crawfish, and any other crustacean I can find fresh. Oh, and I like lots of garlic!"

An especially bright culinary moment was serving Mimi Sheraton (New York food critic) and three guests on a busy night without knowing of her presence.

"I was told later that it was her most enjoyable dining experience in at least a year."

Blank likes junk food in the form of a huge, greasy hamburger with absolutely everything on it.

Aphorisms of Jeffrey Blank

1. Except for the basics, don't follow the recipes — follow your instincts and tastebuds.
2. The harder I work, the more luck I seem to have.
3. The best shortcut is to make hollandaise in the food processor.
4. Dining in a classic restaurant is total decadence.
5. Music fires up the clean-up crews and saves labor costs.

CHEF JEFFREY BLANK

Hudson's on the Bend
3509 Ranch Road 620
Austin (512) 266-1369

Menu

Eggplant Hudson

Sanford Sauvignon Blanc or McDowel Fumé Blanc

Pheasant and Tortilla Soup

Callaway Chenin Blanc or Simi Rosé of Cabernet Sauvignon

Hudson's on the Bend Smoked Shrimp and
Avocado Quesidilla with Corn Pudding and Pico de Gallo

Stag's Leap Sauvignon Blanc or Clos du Bois Chardonnay

Val Verde Port Parfait

Coffee

Val Verde Don Louis Tawny Port

Scharffenberger Brut

EGGPLANT HUDSON

Serves 4

1 medium eggplant
Buttermilk for dipping
Flour for dusting
1/2 cup ricotta cheese
2 10-oz. bags of spinach, lightly blanched in water. Rinse and cool with water. Strain all water out of cooked spinach and chop fine.
Toss spinach with following mixed ingredients:

3 whole eggs (raw)
1/2 tbsp. minced fresh garlic
2 tbsp. minced shallots
1 tbsp. fresh basil (minced)
1 tbsp. minced fresh oregano
3/4 tbsp. minced fresh thyme
1/2 tbsp. whole pepper
3/4 tbsp. salt (or to taste)

Peel medium eggplant and slice lengthwise — nose to heel, 1/4-inch thick. Dip in buttermilk and dust in flour. Sauté in pan with clarified butter over medium-high heat on both sides or until light golden brown. Cool in refrigerator.

Take cooled eggplant and place ricotta cheese and spinach mix (4–5 tbsp.) on top. Roll eggplant around spinach stuffing. Serve atop a rich tomato sauce (Hudson Tomato Sauce) with sprinkles of ground parmesan cheese and basil sprig garnish.

HUDSON TOMATO SAUCE

Yield: 10 oz.

1/2 lb. bacon, sautéed, diced to 1/4 inch (reserve 2 tbsp. drippings)

2 large white onions, diced to 1/4 inch
Red cooking wine

Sauté onion in bacon drippings until clear. Add 1/2 bottle good red cooking wine to onions. Reduce 30%. Now add:

6 cups roma tomatoes, skinned and diced
1 1/2 cups tomato juice
1 1/2 cups tomato paste
3 tbsp. fresh oregano
3 tbsp. fresh sweet basil
3 tbsp. fresh marjoram
2 tbsp. fresh thyme
1 1/2 tbsp. white pepper
4 bay leaves
3 tbsp. diced garlic
1/2 cup sugar
1 1/2 tbsp. salt, or to taste

Cook over low heat for 3 hours. Refrigerate and save what you don't use.

PHEASANT AND TORTILLA SOUP

Serves 4

5 cups rich pheasant stock (or rich chicken stock)
1/2 cup fresh corn
1/2 cup diced onion
1/2 cup diced celery
1/2 cup diced carrots
1 cup chopped cilantro
4 serrano peppers, diced
1 cup lime juice
1 1/2 cups pulled pheasant meat

Heat stock and add remaining ingredients. Salt to taste and simmer for 45 minutes. Serve in crock with strips of fried corn tortillas across top with Monterey Jack cheese melted on top (use broiler in oven to melt cheese).

Garnish with slices of fresh avocado on top of cheese.

Refrigerate extra soup — it's great for New Year's Day parties or holiday football games.

HUDSON'S ON THE BEND SMOKED SHRIMP AND AVOCADO QUESIDILLA

Serves 8

Quesidilla mix

6 oz. goat cheese (Larson Farms)
4 oz. grated Jack cheese
4 oz. sour cream
1/4 tsp. cayenne pepper
1/4 tsp. basil, whole leaf
1/4 tsp. oregano, whole leaf
1/4 tsp. thyme, whole leaf
1/4 tsp. salt
2 tbsp. lemon juice

Combine in bowl. Set until at room temperature and then mix until smooth.

Smoked shrimp

24 shrimp, peeled and deveined
1 cup sour cream
4 tbsp. lemon juice
2 tbsp. paprika
1/4 cup white wine
1/4 tsp. cayenne pepper
1/2 tsp. salt

Mix shrimp with other ingredients. Smoke in a cool to warm smoker until medium rare. Assemble onto 8 tortillas, spoon quesidilla mix over, and warm to melt cheese.

CORN PUDDING

Serves 20

Step one
Mix:

1 1/2 cups flour
1/2 cup sugar
5 tbsp. baking powder
3/4 tbsp. salt or seasoning salt
1/2 tbsp. cayenne pepper

Step two
Mix well:

10 whole eggs
1 cup heavy cream
1/3 lb. of butter, melted
2 cans cream corn (8 oz.)

Step three
Mix:

Green bell pepper
Red bell pepper
Anaheim pepper
2 lbs. cut corn

Remove seeds from peppers and dice to 1/4-inch size. Mix with corn.

Combine the mixed ingredients from steps one, two, and three. Using a large, flat casserole pan, coat with butter and dust with flour. Add pudding mixture until only 1 1/2 inches deep. Use another pan for any extra pudding. Preheat oven to 375 degrees. Cook pudding 40 to 45 minutes or until pudding is golden brown and firm.

PICO DE GALLO

Yield: 8 oz.

3 roma tomatoes, diced 1/4-inch
1 large white onion, diced 1/4-inch
3 to 4 serrano peppers, seeded and minced
1 large juicy lime, squeezed
4 tbsp. finely diced cilantro
1/4 tsp. salt

Combine all ingredients and refrigerate for 2 hours before serving.

VAL VERDE PORT PARFAIT

Select your favorite vanilla and/or coffee ice cream. Soak 1 cup raisins or golden currants in 2 cups Val Verde Don Louis Tawny Port until plump.

In a parfait container, arrange a scoop of vanilla ice cream, then port and fruit, then a scoop of coffee ice cream, and top with port and fruit.

Norbert Brandt

Norbert Brandt, born April 14, 1953, in Hamburg, West Germany, always wanted to be named Chef Brandt. For him, the only birthday cake is real Black Forest cake.

His culinary training took place in Germany, Switzerland, Canada, Singapore, and San Francisco — a total of twenty-two years in the kitchen.

"My most esteemed honor was to prepare an official state dinner given by President Reagan in California to honor Queen Elizabeth," he says.

Brandt loves to create desserts, but his favorite dish to eat is dry-cured sausage and meat and cheeses with a good Cabernet Sauvignon. To him, junk food is anything produced for fast, mass feeding. And yes, he does eat it.

"My best culinary moment was the opening day of Louie B's restaurant and the most fun event was our first New Year's Eve party. After everything was over at Louie B's, we really let loose."

Brandt likes to spend his days off with his family — swimming, cooking barbecue, watching a good movie, and training his German shepherd.

Aphorisms of Norbert Brandt

1. Set one goal at a time; make it realistic and work hard to achieve it.
2. In private or professional life, if you do something, do it right or don't do it at all.
3. Try as many restaurants as is possible.

CHEF NORBERT BRANDT

Louie B's
301 East Sixth Street
Austin (512) 476-1997

Menu

Sautéed Gulf Shrimp Burrito with Three-cheese Sauce

Matanzas Creek Sauvignon Blanc or
Wimberley Valley Cellar Select White Table Wine

Lamb's Lettuce with Lamb Sausage and Balsam Vinaigrette

Merlion Chevrier or Renaissance Dry White Riesling

Roast Pork Tenderloin with Braised Garlic and Lentil Stew

Round Hill Merlot or Messina Hof Barrel Fermented Chardonnay

Flourless Chocolate Cake on Hot Coffee Bean Fudge Sauce

Coffee

Moyer Texas Sparkling Wine

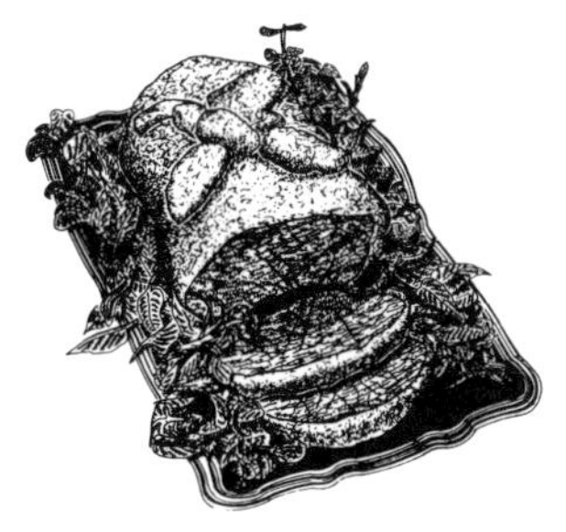

SAUTÉED GULF SHRIMP BURRITO WITH THREE-CHEESE SAUCE

Serves 4

2 tbsp. shallots, chopped
$^1/_2$ cup red bell peppers, cubed fine
1 tbsp. poblano peppers, cubed fine
$^1/_2$ tsp. jalapeño peppers, chopped (seedless)
$^1/_2$ cup celery, cubed fine
2 tbsp. butter
12 medium to large fresh Gulf shrimp, peeled and deveined
1 cup dry white wine
1 tsp. flavored rice vinegar
2 oz. Young Texas Hill Country goat cheese crumbles
3 oz. Cheddar cheese, shredded
2 oz. Monterey Jack cheese, shredded
$1^1/_2$ cups heavy whipping cream
1 tbsp. cilantro, chopped
Salt and pepper to taste
4 soft flour tortillas

Sauté the shallots, the peppers, and celery with the butter for 2 to 3 minutes over a medium heat. Add the shrimp and sauté for 2 to 3 minutes more. Then deglaze the pan with white wine and rice vinegar. Let simmer for 1 minute. Remove shrimp and keep warm.

Mix in the 3 cheeses over low heat by stirring constantly. Add cream and let simmer for 2 to 3 minutes. Add cilantro, salt and pepper to taste. Remove sauce from heat.

Heat the tortillas on an open grill; place 3 shrimp in the middle of each tortilla and cover them with the sauce. Fold the tortilla into a half-moon and serve.

LAMB'S LETTUCE WITH LAMB SAUSAGE AND BALSAM VINAIGRETTE

Serves 4

Lamb's lettuce, well washed

Vinaigrette:
2 tbsp. balsam vinaigrette
1 tbsp. flavored rice vinegar
1 tsp. fresh basil, chopped
1 tsp. shallots, chopped
Chives, coarsely cut
1 tsp. parsley, chopped
1 tbsp. honey
$^1/_2$ cup olive oil
$^1/_2$ cup peanut oil
Salt, to taste
Black pepper, to taste

Sausage:

20 oz. lamb shoulder meat with 10% fat
1 medium onion, chopped
1/2 tsp. fennel seeds
1 tbsp. garlic, chopped
1/2 tsp. thyme, chopped
1/2 tsp. black pepper
2 bay leaves
1/4 tsp. rosemary
1/2 cup heavy whipping cream
3 whole eggs
Salt and pepper, to taste
1 large Idaho baked potato, cooked and cubed

Balsam vinaigrette:
Combine the balsam vinegar with the rice vinegar; add the basil, shallots, chives, parsley, and honey. Mix well and then slowly add the olive oil and peanut oil. Season with salt and black pepper. Let the vinaigrette rest overnight.

For sausage:
Cube the lamb shoulders into 1-inch cubes. Then mix with the onions, fennel seeds, garlic, thyme, black pepper, bay leaves, and rosemary. Mix well and let marinate overnight in a covered bowl.

Pass the meat through a medium coarse meat grinder. Add the cream, eggs, and salt and pepper. Mix well. Then add in the cubed cooked potato. Mix well and make 2-inch patties. Sauté the sausage on medium heat until done. Arrange lamb and lettuce on plate and sprinkle with vinaigrette.

ROAST PORK TENDERLOIN WITH BRAISED GARLIC AND LENTIL STEW

Serves 4

Pork tenderloin:

1/2 tbsp. garlic
1/2 cup olive oil
1 tsp. coriander
1/2 tsp. rosemary
1 tsp. thyme leaves
1 tsp. black crushed pepper

Combine all ingredients and then marinate the pork for 24 hours.

Lentil stew:

1 cup garlic cloves, peeled
2 tbsp. olive oil
1 cup onions, cubed
1 tsp. fresh thyme, chopped
2 bay leaves
3 cups dry lentils, soak 24 hours
2 cups chicken stock
1 tbsp. red wine vinegar
1 1/2 tsp. sugar
1/2 tsp. black pepper
1/2 cup cream
Salt to taste
1/4 lb. soft butter
1 1/2 tsp. cilantro, fresh chopped
Roasted red bell pepper to garnish

Sauté the garlic cloves in olive oil for 3 to 4 minutes or until slightly brown. Then add the onions and sauté again for 3 or 4 minutes. Add the thyme, bay leaves, lentils, chicken stock, vinegar, sugar, pepper, cream, and salt. Cover the casserole and let simmer over low heat for 30 minutes or until lentils are slightly overcooked. Slowly mix in the soft butter. At the end, mix in the cilantro. Roast the pork on the mesquite wood until medium well, then slice and place onto lentils. Garnish with roasted red bell peppers.

FLOURLESS CHOCOLATE CAKE ON HOT COFFEE BEAN FUDGE SAUCE

Serves 12

Cake

7 oz. semisweet chocolate, crumbled
4 oz. butter
2 tbsp. Grand Marnier
1/2 tsp. vanilla extract
1/2 tbsp. almond powder
5 egg yolks
5 egg whites
1 cup sugar

In a bowl, put chocolate, butter, Grand Marnier, vanilla, and almond powder. Melt ingredients over double boiler. Remove from heat as soon as melted and whip lightly. In a separate bowl, whip the egg yolks and half the sugar until a ribbon is formed, about 5 minutes. Blend eggs into chocolate and mix well. In another bowl, whip egg whites vigorously. Slowly, add the rest of the sugar, whipping until lightly firm. Fold into chocolate by hand. Use a 10-inch mold and bake cake at 275 degrees for 1 hour and 20 minutes. Put sauce on cake and serve.

Hot coffee bean fudge sauce

12 oz. sugar
4 oz. brandy
3 oz. lemon juice
4 envelopes instant Sanka coffee
1 tbsp. vanilla extract
3 cups sour cream
4 oz. Kahlua liquer

Caramelize the sugar until light brown. Mix brandy and lemon juice with coffee powder and vanilla extract. When the sugar is still boiling hot, add the brandy mixture, but make sure the flame is off. Mix well and bring back to a boil. When the sugar is melted, add the sour cream and mix well. At the end, add the Kahlua.

Thierry Burklé

"Instead of a birthday cake, I like a bottle of Champagne," says Thierry Burklé. "I enjoy the other courses of a meal too much to save room for a sweet."

Born in Paris, France, on May 21, 1954, Burklé's culinary training was in the family restaurant business in France and Washington, D.C., at the Rive Gauche.

He wears tennis shoes in the kitchen.

"Rather than a favorite dish to prepare, it's the marriage of flavors and creating lightness of foods that I enjoy," he says. "I'm an optimist and don't think about the worst or best of things. I don't look for disasters. The most fun event is having happy customers."

He believes the best shortcut in cooking is to be simple and the most successful substitute is to use fresh ingredients.

Aphorisms of Thierry Burklé

1. Master the combinations and marry the flavors.
2. Nothing takes the place of quality.
3. Some tradition must be retained.
4. Make every day a recipe of happiness.

CHEF THIERRY BURKLÉ

L'Etoile
6106 Broadway at Albany
San Antonio
(512) 826-4551

Menu

Crab Salad a la Geisha

Beringer Sauvignon Blanc or
Mirassou Family Selection White Burgundy

Fresh Norwegian Salmon Marinated with Dill

Iron Horse Sauvignon Blanc or Fall Creek Chardonnay

Baked Lobster in Shell with its Coral (Roe)
with Crab, Blended with Herbs, Spices, and Butter

Cambria Chardonnay or Jekel Chardonnay

Two Black and White Chocolate Layers
with Raspberry Sauce

Coffee

Domaine Chandon Brut

CRAB SALAD A LA GEISHA

Serves 4

Salad

4 oz. cleaned and cooked Blue Crab meat
2 oz. Belgium endive
4 oz. grated carrots
4 medium shrimp, cooked and peeled
1 oz. bean sprouts
1 medium tomato
1/2 cup pink grapefruit, peeled and diced
1 tsp. chopped parsley

Dressing

4 tbsp. cottage cheese
1 tsp. chopped basil
1 tbsp. ketchup
1 tbsp. Dijon mustard
1 oz. fresh grapefruit juice
1 squeezed lemon
1 tbsp. olive oil
Pinch of salt and pepper

In a large bowl, mix all the crab salad ingredients gently in order to preserve the texture and appearance. Mix the dressing ingredients and add to salad, according to taste.

LE SALMON FRAIS MARINE A L'ANETH ET SA CREME FOUETTE

(Fresh Norwegian Salmon Marinated with Dill)

Serves 4

16 oz. of Norwegian Salmon filets
1 cup olive oil
2 tsp. dill
3 limes
1 tbsp. cayenne pepper
1 cup heavy cream
Pinch of salt

Marinate salmon in olive oil, 1 tsp. dill, juice of 2 limes, and 1/2 tsp. cayenne pepper for 4 hours. Whip heavy cream with whisk until slightly stiff, and then add remaining dill, lime juice, cayenne pepper, and salt.

Spread cream mixture in the center of 4 dinner plates. Slice the salmon thinly and lay it over mixture. Brush salmon lightly with remaining marinade sauce.

LE HOMARD FARCIS AU CRABE ET AROMATES

(Baked Lobster in Shell with its Coral (Roe) with Crab, Blended with Herbs, Spices, and Butter)

Serves 2

2 lobsters (1 1/2 lbs. each)
6 tsp. butter
1/2 tsp. cayenne pepper
1/2 garlic clove
2 tsp. chopped basil
3 tsp. chopped shallots
2 oz. fresh lump crab meat
2 oz. Alaskan King Crab
1/5 cup cognac
1 cup Lobster Sauce (recipe follows)
2 tsp. heavy cream
1/2 cup Beurre Blanc Sauce (recipe follows)
Salt and pepper to taste

Preheat oven or broiler to 375 degrees. Cut each lobster in half and remove the claws. Discard intestines, clean the head, set aside the coral. Put lobsters in sauté pan.

Coral preparation:

Mix 3 tsp. butter, cayenne pepper, garlic, 1 tsp. chopped basil, 1 tsp. chopped shallots, 1/2 squeeze of lemon, and the coral.

Brush coral mixture over lobsters. Put lobsters in preheated oven or broiler for 12 minutes. Brush lobsters occasionally with coral mixture to keep them moist.

Crab stuffing preparation:

Sauté the remaining shallots in 3 tsp. butter. Add the 2 types of crab and flambé with cognac. Add remaining 1 tsp. basil, 1/2 cup of Lobster Sauce, and 2 tsp. heavy cream. Cook for 5 minutes and set aside.

Claw preparation:

Bring 1 qt. water to a boil; add the 4 claws and boil for 12 minutes. Remove claws from water, crack the shells and gently remove the flesh in one piece.

Remove lobsters from sauté pan. Mix 1/3 cup each Lobster Sauce and Beurre Blanc Sauce in pan and simmer for 2 minutes. Stuff head of lobster with the crab stuffing.

Put lobster on 2 plates and top with sauce. Place claws at head of lobster to decorate.

Lobster sauce

1 chopped medium onion
1/2 cup chopped celery
1/2 cup chopped carrots
1/4 cup tomato paste
3 lobster heads
1 cup cognac
1 qt. fish stock (or clam juice)
1/4 cup rice, uncooked
Salt and cayenne pepper to taste

Cook onions, celery, and carrots in large pan with olive oil until transparent. Add tomato paste and lobster heads and heat. Deglaze with brandy. Add stock and rice, then boil for 30 minutes. Grind and strain; boil again. Salt and pepper to taste.

Beurre blanc sauce

1/4 cup white wine
1/4 cup white vinegar
2 tbsp. shallots
1 cup heavy cream
1/2 cup butter

In skillet, cook wine, vinegar, and shallots until liquid is reduced. Add cream and heat until cream is reduced by half. Add butter and simmer. Do not let this mixture boil. Set aside.

LA TERRINE AUX DEUX CHOCOLATES AUX CULIS DE FRAMBOISES FRAICHES

(Two Black and White Chocolate Layers with Raspberry Sauce)

Serves 6

4 oz. ground white chocolate
4 oz. ground semisweet chocolate
1 1/2 gelatine sheets
1/2 cup heavy cream
6 egg whites

Melt each chocolate separately in a double boiler. Put the gelatine sheets in cold water to soften. Bring the cream to a boil and then add the softened gelatine sheets. Remove mixture from the heat and let it cool.

Split mixture evenly and mix with each chocolate. Whip 3 egg whites and add slowly to the white chocolate with a spatula. Repeat this step using the dark chocolate.

Butter the inside of 6 small glasses. Layer the chocolates (dark on bottom, light on top). Chill for 6 hours. Remove from molds and serve with raspberry sauce.

Robert Del Grande

A native of San Francisco, California (born November 1, 1954), Robert Del Grande is a witty, easygoing sort of guy who began cooking as a diversion. Having just completed a Ph.D. in biochemistry, he relaxed from that pursuit by working in a friend's restaurant kitchen and ended up owning Cafe Annie.

Chef Del Grande's numerous awards include "Who's Who in Food and Wine in Texas," "*Cook's* magazine's Who's Who in 1987," a *Food & Wine* magazine's choice for Best Young Chefs in 1983, and more.

Among his favorite things are chocolate cake with chocolate frosting for his birthday, cooking and eating polenta, wearing tennis shoes in the kitchen, all his awards, New Year's Eve, looking forward to his best culinary moment, the Texas Hill Country Wine and Food Festival, playing golf and the guitar, and forgotten disasters.

He had fun responding to some questions, which follow.

Q. What did you want to be named?
A. One-eyed Cowboy Bob.

Q. What have fortune tellers told you?
A. Head Southwest.

Q. Most difficult preparation?
A. Poached eggs.

Q. Favorite tip to cooks?
A. Taste is silent.

Q. Best shortcut?
A. Invite friends in to help.

Q. Most successful substitute?
A. Dining out.

Q. Define junk food.
A. Food you store in the attic.

CHEF ROBERT DEL GRANDE

Cafe Annie
1728 Post Oak
Houston
(713) 780-1522

Menu

Squid Soup with Tomato and Chilies

Dry Creek Sauvignon Blanc, Simi Chenin Blanc, or Consentino Crystal Valley Cabernet Franc

Sweet Potato Tamales

Rodney Strong Johannisberg Riesling or Christian Brothers White Zinfandel

Roasted Venison Leg with Dried Red Chilies and Maple

Markham Cabernet Sauvignon, Ravenswood Zinfandel, or De Loach Chardonnay

New York Strip Steak with Avocado Relish and Sweet-n-Sour Steak Sauce and Buttermilk Batter-fried Lumberjack Potatoes

Sausal or Ridge or Charles Krug Cabernet Sauvignon

Pecan and Chocolate Pie with Orange Custard Sauce

Coffee

Culbertson Cuvee de Frontignan

S. Anderson Brut

SQUID SOUP WITH TOMATO AND CHILIES

Serves 4

1 lb. fresh squid, cleaned
2 tomatoes (approximately 20 oz.)
½ onion
2 garlic cloves
2 jalapeños
½ cup chicken broth
2 tbsp. butter
1 tsp. salt
1 tsp. sugar
1 tsp. lime juice
1 bunch cilantro, chopped

Salsa

1 tomato, coarsely diced
½ onion, finely chopped
1 jalapeño, seeded and finely chopped
½ bunch cilantro, chopped
1 tsp. lime juice
Salt and pepper to taste

Garnishes

½ cup sour cream
Tomato salsa
Cilantro leaves

To prepare the soup, cut the squid bodies into small strips. Cut the tentacles into quarters. Place the two tomatoes, onion, garlic, and jalapeños in a small roasting pan and cook in a 375-degree oven for 45 minutes or until the tomatoes are well roasted. Transfer the cooked ingredients to a blender. Add the chicken broth and blend until smooth (approximately 1 minute). Reserve.

Melt the butter in a deep sauté pan over medium heat. Add the squid, salt, sugar, and lime juice and and slowly cook. After a few minutes the squid should release some liquid (approximately ½ cup). Add the tomato purée to the squid. Bring to a boil and then simmer the soup for 10 minutes. Just before serving add the chopped cilantro.

Combine all the salsa ingredients and mix well. Salt and pepper to taste.

Ladle hot soup into bowls. Add a dollop of sour cream to the center of each serving. Place some tomato salsa in the center of the sour cream. Garnish with cilantro leaves.

SWEET POTATO TAMALES WITH ANCHO CHILE JAM AND SOUR CREAM

Yield: 12

4 medium sweet potatoes

Tamale dough

8 oz. unsalted butter (slightly softened)
2-3 oz. lard
2 cups cornmeal
1 cup masa harina
1 tsp. baking powder
1 tsp. kosher salt
2 cups chicken stock (strong)
20 dried corn husks (separate and soak in water until moist)

Ancho chile jam

1/2 lb. ancho chilies
3/4 tbsp. vinegar
2 tbsp. honey
1/2 shallot
1 clove garlic
1 1/2 oz. red currant jelly
Pinch of salt
Sour cream

Preheat oven to 400 degrees. Wash sweet potatoes. Pat dry and place on roasting tray and bake for approximately 30 minutes or until soft. Cool.

To prepare tamale dough, combine butter and lard in electric mixer bowl and whip until very light. Combine cornmeal, masa harina, baking powder, and salt. With the mixer running, slowly add the cornmeal mixture and stock alternately. Refrigerate until ready. May be prepared up to a few days in advance.

Allow the tamale dough to warm to room temperature so that it is soft enough to spread. Lay soaked corn husks on clean flat surface. Using a pastry knife spread an even layer of dough (3–4 tbsp.) across the center of each husk. Spoon sweet potato (approximately 2 tbsp.) into center of the dough. Using the sides of the husk, bring the edges of the dough together so that the potato is encased in dough. Fold one edge of the husk over the other and tie the ends of the husks tightly together using thin strips of husk.

Meanwhile, soak the ancho chilies in water until soft. Purée the chilies in a blender with the vinegar, honey, shallot, garlic and jelly until very smooth and thick. Adjust honey or vinegar to balance pepperiness and tart-sweetness. Salt to taste.

Place tamales in the tray of a steamer and gently steam for 10–15 minutes or until the tamales are puffy and light. Split the tamales open and garnish with the ancho chile jam and sour cream.

ROASTED VENISON LEG WITH DRIED RED CHILIES AND MAPLE

Serves 8

1 whole Axis venison leg (8 to 10 lbs.), trimmed

Marinade

12 ancho chilies
4 garlic cloves
1/2 red onion
1 oz. pure maple syrup
1/2 cup honey
1 tsp. kosher salt

Soak the ancho chilies in a minimum amount of water until soft. Reserve the chile water.

Transfer the chilies, garlic, onion, and one cup of chile water to a blender and purée until a smooth paste is formed. Add additional water if necessary. The chile purée should have the consistency of a thick ketchup.

Add the maple syrup, honey, and salt and purée until blended. This paste will keep covered in a refrigerator for up to 2 weeks.

Brush the venison leg with the marinade, season with cracked pepper, and allow to marinate overnight.

Roast the venison in a 350-degree oven for approximately 1 1/2 hours (10–15 minutes per pound for medium rare). Allow the leg to rest for 20 minutes in a warm (150-degree) oven before carving.

Sauce

8 ancho chilies
4 cascabel chilies
2 chipotle chilies
1 qt. venison or chicken stock
1 oz. pure maple syrup
1/2 oz. unsweetened baking chocolate
Juice from 1/2 lime
Kosher salt
Fresh ground pepper
4 oz. unsalted butter (soft)

Soak the chilies until soft in 2 cups of the stock. Purée the soft chilies with the stock in a blender until smooth. Transfer the purée to a saucepan and add the remaining stock. Bring to a slow boil and reduce until the sauce is slightly thickened.

Add the maple syrup, chocolate, and lime juice and blend. Salt and pepper to taste. Keep the sauce warm until ready.

Just before serving, whip in the butter in small nuggets until the butter is emulsified into the sauce. Because of the unpredictability of the chilies, more or less maple syrup may be needed to balance the spiciness of the sauce.

NEW YORK STRIP STEAK WITH AVOCADO RELISH AND SWEET-N-SOUR STEAK SAUCE AND BUTTERMILK BATTER-FRIED LUMBERJACK POTATOES

Serves 6

6 New York strip steaks
4 medium Idaho potatoes, roasted until done and cooled to room temperature

Avocado papaya relish

1 red bell pepper
1 yellow bell pepper
2 poblano chilies
1 red onion, sliced
2 garlic cloves
3 to 6 tbsp. cilantro tops, roughly chopped
2 avocados
1 papaya
Lime
Salt and pepper

Steak sauce

1 orange (zest and juice)
6 plum tomatoes, stemmed and quartered
4 to 6 dried red chiles (ancho), stemmed and seeded
1 small yellow onion, roughly chopped
6 cloves garlic
2 cups white wine vinegar
2 cups water
1 cup brown sugar
1/4 cup achiote block or seeds (annatto seeds) — optional
Salt and pepper to taste

Buttermilk batter

3 shallots, finely minced
2 whole eggs
1 tbsp. finely minced fresh rosemary
1/2 to 3/4 cup buttermilk
3/4 cup all-purpose flour
2 tsp. baking powder
1 tsp. kosher salt
1 tsp. cracked black pepper

Relish (3 cups):

Char the skin of the bell peppers and poblano chiles over a charcoal grill. Peel and seed the chiles and peppers.

Slow grill the onion slices and garlic cloves. Combine the grilled ingredients in a food processor and briefly process to yield a rough-cut relish. Add the cilantro and mix well.

Peel and seed the avocados and papaya and cut into a small dice.

Combine the diced avocado and papaya with the pepper relish. Add the juice of 1 lime and mix (do not overmix). Salt and pepper to taste.

Steak sauce (2 qts.):

Zest the orange (use a potato peeler to remove just the outer skin without any of the membrane attached) and mince. Peel remaining membrane from the orange and quarter. Remove any seeds.

Combine the orange and zest with the remainder of the sauce ingredients in a sauce pot. Bring the liquid to a boil and then simmer for approximately 30 minutes or until the ingredients are very soft. Allow to cool.

Transfer the ingredients with the liquid to a blender and purée until smooth. Purée should be of commercial steak sauce consistency. If not, reduce liquid by simmering. Salt and pepper to taste. (Note: Sauce can be refrigerated and stored for 2 weeks.)

Buttermilk batter and potatoes:

Combine the shallot, egg, rosemary, and buttermilk and mix well.

Sift together the flour, baking powder, and salt and pepper. Stir the flour mixture into the buttermilk-egg mixture. Do not overmix. Batter should be thick enough to evenly coat potatoes.

Heat oil for deep frying to 350 degrees. Slice the roasted potatoes lengthwise into quarters. Dip the quarters into the buttermilk batter. Fry the potatoes until the batter is golden brown. Drain.

To serve:

Grill or panbroil the steak to the desired doneness. Spoon the steak sauce onto the bottom of dinner plates to just cover. Place the steaks on the sauce. Spoon the avocado papaya relish over the steak. Serve with the fried potatoes.

PECAN AND CHOCOLATE PIE WITH ORANGE CUSTARD SAUCE

Yield: two 9-inch pies

Pie dough

1½ lbs. all-purpose flour
Pinch of sugar
Pinch of salt
1 lb. chilled butter, cut into small cubes
4 oz. cold water

Pecan pie mixture

8 whole eggs
4 egg yolks
Small pinch of salt
2 tbsp. pure vanilla
1 cup brown sugar
1 cup granulated sugar
1½ cups dark corn syrup
1½ cups light corn syrup
4 tbsp. melted butter
3 cups pecans, chopped
8 oz. semisweet chocolate, broken into small pieces

Orange custard sauce

4 oranges
Zest from 4 oranges, finely minced
½ cup sugar
1 cup milk
1 cup cream
6 egg yolks
2 tbsp. Grand Marnier

Raspberry purée

1 pt. fresh raspberries
¼ cup sugar
Water

Pie dough:

Combine the flour, pinch of sugar and salt, and the cubes of cold butter and mix just until the butter is coated with flour. Add the cold water and mix until a rough dough is formed. Do not overmix; small pieces of butter should be visible. Divide the dough into two pieces. Roll out each piece into a circle approximately ¼-inch thick. Place the dough into 9-inch pie dishes and form a fluted edge around the rim. Refrigerate the dough in the pie dishes until well chilled.

Pecan mixture:

Combine the whole eggs, egg yolks, salt, and vanilla and mix well. Add the brown sugar and granulated sugar and whip until the sugar is nearly dissolved. Add the dark and light corn syrup, melted butter, and chopped pecans and mix until well incorporated.

Sprinkle the pieces of chocolate evenly over the bottom of the chilled pie shells. Pour the pecan mixture into the shells. Bake at 375 for 15 minutes then lower the heat to 300 and bake until the pies are set. Allow to cool before slicing.

Orange custard sauce:

Combine the juice from the oranges with the minced zest and the sugar and boil to reduce to 1/2 cup. Add the milk and the cream and bring to a boil. Lower the heat. Whip the egg yolks into the hot liquid. Slowly heat the mixture while constantly stirring until the custard lightly thickens. Add the Grand Marnier to finish the sauce. Cool to room temperature.

Raspberry purée:

Place the raspberries and sugar in a blender and purée. Add just enough water to form a purée that is the consistency of the orange custard sauce.

Service:

Slice the pie into 10 pieces. Spoon some orange custard sauce onto each dessert plate. Place a slice of pecan pie in the center of each plate. Drizzle some raspberry purée over the sauce. Dust each plate with powdered sugar.

Optional: Serve with vanilla ice cream.

Dean Fearing

Dean Fearing was born in Ashland, Kentucky, February 7, 1955. His culinary training began with a cooking school degree from Jefferson Community College and he graduated from the Culinary Institute of America (CIA) in 1978.

Some favorites of Fearing include Christmas, wearing boots in the kitchen, cooking and eating pasta, playing the guitar, doing "Meals on Wheels" with Wolfgang Puck in Los Angeles, eating at the restaurants of all his friends, and German chocolate cake on his birthday.

He doesn't like fortune tellers. He doesn't want to know what's going to happen because he likes the sense of discovery.

"I guess my most esteemed honor was being interviewed to be a chef at the White House. But it was also an honor to be one of the pioneers in Southwestern cuisine, starting it with Anne Greer, Robert Del Grande, and Stephan Pyles," he smiled. "We didn't know how it would develop."

Fearing was awarded "Who's Who in Food and Wine in Texas," selected as one of *Food & Wine* magazine's Top Ten Young Chefs, named in *Cook's* magazine Who's Who in 1987, among others.

When asked to name his best culinary moment, Fearing said, "Where do I begin! Graduating from CIA was one. Being accepted as the saucier at La Maisonette in Cincinnati for my first job. My first job as chef for Agnew's Restaurant and getting five stars after we'd only been open for six weeks. Being chef at the Mansion. I was one of the first employees at the Mansion when it opened in 1980 and it was wonderful to come back as chef."

His most difficult preparation is making the "old-time" garnishes and patés by the classic French techniques.

And junk food he defines as Domino's pizza — he orders it constantly and puts fresh grated cheese and ground black pepper on the top.

Aphorisms of Dean Fearing

---

1. A tip for cooks is to use chicken stock as a base for all soups. It works better and is less trouble than fish stock.
2. The best shortcut is to not use cream, butter, and fats.
3. My philosophy is common sense and good cooking.
4. Whistle while you work, and sing.

CHEF DEAN FEARING

Mansion on Turtle Creek
2821 Turtle Creek Boulevard
Dallas
(214) 559-2100

Menu

Southwest Corn Chowder

Llano Estacado Chardonnay or
Kendall-Jackson Clear Lake Sauvignon Blanc

Snapper with Orange-Horseradish Crust and
Thai Shrimp Salad

Cakebread Sauvignon Blanc or Merryvale Chardonnay

Barbecued Glazed Loin of Rabbit
with Ancho-Smoked Bacon Chili

Lyeth White Table Wine or Clos du Bois Briarcrest

Phoenix Texas Star with Gingerbread

Coffee

Iron Horse Brut

SOUTHWEST CORN CHOWDER

Serves 6

6 large ears sweet corn
1 tsp. corn oil
2 onions, cut into medium dice
2 cloves garlic, chopped
1 1/2 poblano chilies, seeded and chopped into medium dice
2 serrano chilies, seeded and chopped
3 cups chicken stock
2 cups heavy cream
Salt to taste
1 tbsp. lime juice, approximately
1 small baking potato, peeled and cut into medium dice
1/2 cup jicama, peeled and cut into medium dice
1/4 red bell pepper, seeded and membranes removed, cut into medium dice
1/4 yellow bell pepper, seeded and membranes removed, cut into medium dice
1 tbsp. finely chopped fresh cilantro

Shuck corn, remove silk, and cut kernels from cob. Set aside 3/4 cup. Heat oil in a heavy saucepan over medium heat. Stir in remaining corn kernels and onions. Sauté for about 10 minutes or until onions are soft and juices have cooked down. Do not brown. Add garlic, 1 chopped poblano, 1 chopped serrano chili, and chicken stock. Bring to a boil, stirring frequently. Reduce heat and simmer for 20 minutes. Add heavy cream for last 2 minutes of simmer. Remove from heat. Pour soup into a blender and blend until very smooth. Season to taste with salt and lime juice. Set aside and keep warm.

Fill a large pot three-quarters full with water. Bring to a boil. Season lightly with salt. Add potato and cook for 2 minutes. Add reserved 3/4 cup corn kernels and cook for 2 minutes. Add jicama, bell peppers, and remaining diced poblano and serrano chilies; cook for 2 minutes.

Drain vegetables and immediately fold into warm soup. Pour equal portions into six warm soup bowls. Sprinkle an equal amount of chopped cilantro on each and serve immediately.

SNAPPER WITH ORANGE-HORSERADISH CRUST AND THAI SHRIMP SALAD

Serves 4

1 cup dry bread crumbs
2 tbsp. finely grated fresh horseradish
$1^{1}/_{2}$ tbsp. finely grated orange peel
1 clove garlic, minced
4 7-oz. snapper filets, trimmed of bone and dark membrane
Salt to taste
3 tbsp. peanut oil
1 tsp. sesame oil
Thai Shrimp Salad (recipe follows)

Preheat oven to 375 degrees. In a medium bowl, combine crumbs, horseradish, orange peel, and garlic. Spread mixture on a small plate or wax paper. Season snapper filets lightly with salt, then press each filet into crumb mixture, making sure both sides are completely covered.

Heat oils over medium heat in an ovenproof sauté pan large enough to hold filets in a single layer. Carefully place filets in pan so as not to knock off crumbs. Cook 1 to 2 filets at a time for easier handling. Cook for 1 to 2 minutes to brown crust, but do not burn or blacken.

When all filets are brown on one side, arrange them, uncooked side down, in sauté pan and place in preheated oven. Bake for about 5 minutes or just until fish is firm in the middle. Place a snapper filet on each of four warm dinner plates. Place Thai Shrimp Salad alongside fish, allowing 4 shrimp halves per serving. Dressing from salad should spread to cover the bottom of the plate. Add a bit more dressing, if necessary, and serve immediately.

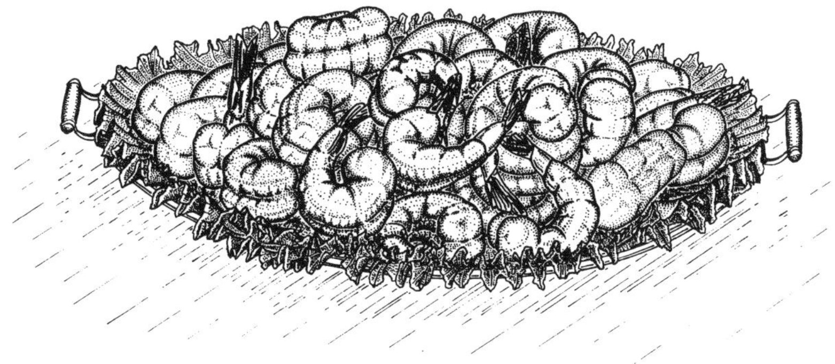

Thai shrimp salad

1/2 red bell pepper, seeded and membranes removed
1/2 yellow bell pepper, seeded and membranes removed
1 cup very thin vertical strips red onion
1/4 cup loosely packed very small whole fresh mint leaves, stems removed
1/4 cup basil leaves
1/4 cup loosely packed cilantro leaves, stems removed
1 clove garlic, minced
2 shallots, minced
1 1/2 tbsp. finely grated fresh ginger
2 Thai chilies, minced
1/2 cup fish sauce (Thai style)
1/2 cup sweet rice wine vinegar
1/2 cup chicken stock
1 tsp. sesame oil
1 tsp. black soy sauce
Juice of 2 limes to taste
Salt to taste
1 tbsp. dark sesame oil
8 medium shrimp, peeled and deveined

Cut pepper vertically into thin strips. Place strips of onion, peppers, mint, basil, and cilantro leaves in a large bowl with ice water to cover. This is very important because it ensures that the vegetables will stay crisp.

In a small bowl, combine garlic, shallots, ginger, Thai chilies, fish sauce, vinegar, chicken stock, sesame oil, and soy sauce, whisking to blend. Season to taste with lime juice and salt. Cover and set aside.

Heat dark sesame oil in a large sauté pan over medium-high heat. Add shrimp and lightly season to taste with salt. Stir-fry shrimp just until firm and no longer translucent. Remove from pan, slice in half lengthwise, and keep warm.

Drain vegetables and herbs, making sure all excess moisture is removed. Place in a large bowl. Gather ends together loosely and gently twirl several times, being careful not to crush the leaves.

Add shrimp and pour dressing over. Toss lightly to combine and coat ingredients with dressing. This salad must be assembled at the last moment to retain the crispness of the iced vegetables and herbs.

BARBECUED GLAZED LOIN OF RABBIT WITH ANCHO-SMOKED BACON CHILI

Serves 6

1 rabbit loin
Barbecue Sauce (recipe follows)
Ancho-smoked Bacon Chili Sauce (recipe follows)

Brush rabbit loin with Barbecue Sauce. Sauté in medium sauté pan for approximately 5 minutes, until done. Remove from pan, slice, and serve on Ancho-smoked Bacon Chili.

Barbecue sauce (1 qt.):

To be smoked in smoker for 1½ hours.

1 peeled yellow onion, roughly chopped
2 ribs of celery, roughly chopped
2 carrots, roughly chopped
10 cloves garlic
2 ancho chili pods
2 chipotles
10 sprigs parsley
2 tomatoes, roughly chopped

Add smoked ingredients to:

2 qts. veal demi-glace
2 oz. fruit vinegar
2 oz. light brown sugar
4 oz. tomato ketchup
1 tbsp. dry mustard

Bring all ingredients to a boil and reduce to 1 qt. Then strain mixture. Taste and add salt to taste.

Ancho-smoked bacon chili sauce:

4 strips apple smoked bacon, small dice
1½ medium onions, small dice
1 green bell pepper, small dice
1 yellow bell pepper, small dice
1 red bell pepper, small dice
3 ancho chilies, seeded and soaked in hot water for 15 minutes
2 serrano chilies, seeded and finely chopped
2 cloves garlic, chopped
1½ tbsp. chili powder
1½ tsp. ground cumin
1½ tsp. coriander
1 tsp. paprika
2 tomatoes, diced
4 cups veal stock for beef boullion
2 lbs. diced tenderloin (rabbit)
Salt and pepper to taste
1 tbsp. chopped cilantro

In a medium saucepan, sauté bacon until rendered. Add onions, peppers, and chilies and cook until onions become translucent. Add garlic and spices, then sauté 1 minute. Add tomatoes and brown stock. Simmer gently for ½ hour to 45 minutes until volume is reduced by half.

In a separate pan, sear diced tenderloin until brown. Pour in chili mix, salt, pepper, and cilantro, then simmer 5 minutes and serve.

PHOENIX TEXAS STAR WITH GINGERBREAD

Makes 1 (9 x 13) cake

1 orange, cleaned and sectioned
3 to 4 strawberries
1/2 pint raspberries
1/4 pint blackberries
1 banana, peeled and sliced
Gingerbread (recipe follows)
Glacé (recipe follows)

Glacé

5 egg yolks
2 1/2 oz. sugar
1/2 cup Grand Marnier

Whip together egg yolks and sugar over double boiler until ribbon consistency. Cool slightly and add Grand Marnier. Set aside for future use.

Gingerbread

1/2 cup butter
1/2 cup sugar
1 beaten egg
1 cup molasses
1 cup boiling water
2 1/2 cups all-purpose flour
1 1/2 tsp. baking soda
1 tsp. cinnamon (ground)
1 tsp. ginger (ground)
1/2 tsp. cloves (ground)
1/2 tsp. salt

Cream butter and sugar together; add egg, cream well. Add molasses and boiling water. Sift together remaining ingredients and add to creamed mixture. Pour batter into greased 9 x 13 sheet pan and bake at 350 degrees for approximately 45–50 minutes or until cake tester comes out clean.

Plating of dessert:

Arrange fruit on plate in a circular pattern, using all fruits. Pour glacé over fruit, enough to cover. Lightly brown under a broiler and serve with a slice of warm gingerbread.

Victor Albert Leopold Gielisse

Born in Scheveningen, Netherlands, on June 15 (no year given), Victor Gielisse is delightful to work with because he's thorough, considerate, and organized. He is also long on sensitivity. His favorite celebration is his daughter's birthday.

Chef Gielisse (pronounced Hee-liss-say) has garnered countless awards, but he is most proud of being one of only forty Certified Master Chefs in the U.S. He earned the coveted designation by passing the grueling ten-day examination with the highest score. He wears clogs and a toque in the kitchen, where he spends 90 hours a week.

When asked what he wanted to be named, Chef Gielisse said, "Leo. Actually, this is funny because during the first part of my apprenticeship, I used this name on the application and became known at work as 'Leo.' One day my parents called and asked for Victor and, needless to say, they were surprised."

Gielisse says he is indebted to Chefs Ari Alink, Scholte and Griek, but his best culinary training was at home.

"My mother and father both provided me with love, strength, and education. Without them I could never have gone this far."

His answer to a favorite dish to cook was "Good Lord, there's so much to choose from. I just love to cook. Everything should be handled with the same amount of love and care."

The chef's most embarrassing culinary moment happened on New Year's Eve in 1976 at a banquet in the Carlton Hotel. It concerned 1,100 appetizers of a rabbit galantine with port wine aspic, beautifully presented in a decorative motif. Twenty minutes before dinner, while being transported to the ballroom, a wheel on the trolley carrying it collapsed. Need any more be said?

His best culinary moment was equally dramatic. It happened in 1986 when eighteen nations were competing in the Culinary Olympics and he was on the U.S.A. team that won, for the first time, the Culinary Gold Cup.

Philosophically, Gielisse says, "I strongly believe in the solid principles of cooking. They provide the foundation for all derivations in cuisine. As a professional, I stress that one cannot permit mediocrity. Once one grasps the basics, he is truly not limited in what he can do and can apply all the creativity available. Good cooking depends on many factors, but first and foremost is quality products. Second, we apply the right cooking skills, proper seasoning, proper handling (sanitation and hygiene, correct storage temperature, etc.), and then nutritional balance and presentation. Food is sensual; let it talk for you. Does it have eye appeal? How does it fit in today's market? Will it sell? Is it cost effective? Does the guest receive proper value for his money?"

Aphorisms of Victor Gielisse

---

1. Training never ceases. One should always try to excel, grow and learn, regardless of age.
2. Often the most simple preparation can also be the most difficult.
3. All preparations require skill, knowledge, and concentration.
4. There's no substitute for quality.
5. Work clean and be professional, never mediocre.
6. Solid cooking principles provide the foundation for all derivations in cuisine.

CHEF VICTOR GIELISSE

Actuelle in the Quadrangle
2800 Routh Street
Dallas
(214) 855-0440

Menu

Yellowtail Snapper, Crayfish and Shrimp Sausages with Roasted Orzo and Buckwheat (Kasha), Black Bean Sauce
Kendall-Jackson or Domaine Michel Chardonnay
or Inglenook Sauvignon Blanc

Bear Meat Consommé with Port Wine and Gold Leaf,
Bear Meat Dumplings
Saintsbury Pinot Noir Carneros or Buena Vista Gamay Beaujolais or Grand Cru Cabernet Sauvignon

Texas Pheasant Pockets and Green Apple-Tomatillo Sauce
Ferrari-Carano Chardonnay, Monticello Cabernet Sauvignon, or Rutherford Hill Merlot

Confit of Duck with Gorgonzola Polenta
and Spinach Mousse
Conn Creek Cabernet Sauvignon or Carneros Creek Pinot Noir

Actuelle Fruit Cobbler
Freemark Abbey Edelwein Gold
Coffee
Maison Deutz Brut

YELLOWTAIL SNAPPER, CRAYFISH AND SHRIMP SAUSAGES

Serves 12 appetizers or 6 as main course

6 oz. yellowtail snapper or pike
4 oz. shrimp
4 oz. scallops
2 egg whites
$^3/_4$ cup cream
$^1/_3$ cup shiitake mushrooms, cleaned and sautéed
1 tbsp. dill, chopped
2 tbsp. parsley, chopped
6 oz. scallops, finely diced
3 oz. fresh crayfish, finely diced

Prepare forcemeat with pike or snapper, shrimp, and scallops. Dice fish into small cubes; place in a bowl over ice. Chill Cuisinart bowl and blade. The key to a strong forcemeat depends on all ingredients being of an even temperature: COLD.

Purée fish in chilled Cuisinart at pulse speed for 30 seconds. Stop. Clean sides. Use pulse speed again for 30 seconds. Add unbeaten egg whites and run at regular speed for 45 seconds. Add $^1/_2$ the cream and run for 30 seconds more. Remove from Cuisinart, put mixture in a bowl and place bowl over ice. Fold in the remainder of the cream. Add dill, parsley, mushrooms, diced crayfish and scallops and season with salt and pepper.

The casings used are generally lamb casings from a good, local butcher shop or gourmet section in a supermarket. They come in a solution that needs to be rinsed off with plain water. Then store them in lightly salted water until ready to use.

Use a pastry bag with a long, round nozzle to pipe forcemeat into casings. Tie with string at $3^1/_2$-inch intervals and poach in court bouillon until done. Remove string and serve with Roasted Orzo and Buckwheat (Kasha) and Black Bean Sauce.

Roasted orzo and buckwheat

6 portions

2 oz. dry orzo
2 oz. kasha
1 tbsp. butter
1 oz. egg whites
1 tsp. shallots, chopped
6 oz. chicken stock
Freshly cracked pepper
$1^1/_2$ oz. walnut oil
$1^1/_2$ oz. filberts, chopped
Salt and pepper
Fresh basil
Cilantro

To prepare orzo, boil water with a little salt, add orzo, and cook until tender. Remove, drain, and rinse with cold water. Keep aside.

To prepare kasha, heat butter in sauté pan. Place egg whites in bowl, add kasha and combine. Add the mixture to the hot pan, stirring frequently. Add shallots, pepper, and stock and bring to a boil. Simmer for 10 minutes or until stock is evaporated. Spread on a sheet pan to cool.

In a sauté pan, heat walnut oil and add chopped filberts. Cook until browned and add kasha and orzo. Season with salt, pepper, fresh basil and cilantro.

Black bean sauce

1 tbsp. olive oil
4 oz. tasso ham
1 onion, medium dice
1 leek
1 stalk celery, medium dice
1 carrot
1 serrano chili, chopped
1/2 bunch cilantro, chopped
2 cloves garlic, minced
8 oz. black beans, sorted, soaked overnight
1 gallon chicken stock

Heat oil in stockpot; add tasso and render. Add onions, leeks, celery, and carrot. Cook until tender and add serrano, cilantro, and garlic. Add drained and rinsed beans and stock and bring to a boil. Simmer until beans are tender (for one hour). Blend mixture and adjust seasoning. Add a little stock if the consistency is too thick.

BEAR MEAT CONSOMMÉ WITH PORT WINE AND GOLD LEAF

Serves 10

1 lb. bear meat, lean and ground (substitute beef)
12 egg whites
2 carrots (mince carrots, celery, leek, and onion together)
2 stalks celery
1 stalk leek
1 onion
6 white peppercorns
2 bay leaves
3 sprigs thyme
1 sprig marjoram
1 sprig tarragon
8 mustard seeds
1/2 gallon clear beef consommé
1/2 oz. brandy
3 oz. port
Freshly cracked pepper to taste

For garnish:

10 each of fresh oyster mushrooms (julienne), and various blanched root vegetables (turnip, celeriac, carrot, parsnip, celery, yam, etc.) totaling 10

10 sheets gold leaf

Cilantro, chopped to garnish 10 bowls

Place bear meat and egg whites in a bowl. Add minced vegetables and combine thoroughly. Make sure mixture remains cool, preferably keeping it over ice. Add peppercorns, bay leaves, thyme, marjoram, tarragon, and mustard seeds and combine with bear meat. Fold in cold consommé. Place the mixture in a stock pot and bring to a boil, stirring every minute or two. When egg white starts to congeal and form a raft, reduce heat and simmer slowly for 1$^1/_2$ hours. Carefully pass consommé through a fine, clean cheesecloth. Bring soup to a boil slowly, add brandy and port to taste, and adjust seasoning. Serve in individual bowls. Garnish with root vegetables and Bear Meat Dumplings (see recipe). Float a sheet of gold leaf on top and sprinkle with chopped cilantro.

Bear meat dumplings (serves 10):

8 oz. wild boar meat
8 oz. bear meat (substitute beef)
4 oz. duck or pheasant livers
4 egg whites, unbeaten
$^1/_2$ cup cream
1 tbsp. pieces of lemon-thyme leaves
2 tbsp. pieces of tarragon leaves
2 tbsp. parsley, chopped
Salt and freshly cracked pepper to taste

Grind the meat finely. Place in bowl over ice; fold in unbeaten egg whites and slowly add the cream. Season with salt, pepper, and herbs. Test one dumpling by poaching in stock. Drop mixture from a spoon into simmering court bouillon. Do not boil. Poach until dumpling floats to the surface and turns freely. Adjust seasoning. Prepare the rest of the dumplings. Serve 1 or 2 per soup bowl.

TEXAS PHEASANT POCKETS

Serves 12

4 oz. butter
4 oz. hickory smoked ham, diced
3 oz. diced shallots
4 oz. diced celery
2 cloves minced garlic
3 tbsp. fresh basil
1/2 oz. sherry
1/2 oz. brandy
3 oz. morels (mushrooms), soaked, rinsed, chopped
1/4 lb. wild rice, cooked
1/3 cup yellow corn, cooked
3 oz. tomato concasse
12 pheasant breasts
Salt and pepper to taste
3 sheets lace fat, washed and cleaned (lace fat is a fine, fragile sheet of fat, but it cooks very well and holds the food product in a proper shape; found in butcher shops and meat sections of gourmet food stores)

In a sauté pan, melt butter and add ham, shallots, celery, and garlic. Sauté over low heat until glazed. Add basil, reduce heat; add a little salt and pepper; add sherry and brandy and reduce slightly. Add morels, wild rice, yellow corn, and tomato concasse, combining gently. Remove from heat and spread stuffing on a sheetpan to cool.

Remove skin and gristle from pheasant breasts. Under plastic wrap, gently flatten each with a cleaver. Spread flattened pheasant breasts on a clean work area. Sprinkle with salt and pepper. Place equal amounts of stuffing on the center of each breast and fold into a pocket shape. Wrap each pocket with lace fat. Chill until needed.

To cook, sauté pockets on both sides until evenly browned. Place in 350-degree oven for 10 to 12 minutes. Serve with Green Apple-Tomatillo Sauce.

Green apple-tomatillo sauce

4 tbsp. clarified butter
1 medium onion, cleaned, diced
2 cloves garlic, minced
1/2 jalapeño pepper, cleaned, chopped, seeded
1 lb. tomatillos, cleaned, washed, diced
3 Granny Smith's apples, cleaned, cored, diced
1 qt. chicken stock
1 bunch cilantro, coarsely chopped
4 oz. heavy cream
Salt and pepper
2 oz. apple jack

Heat butter in saucepan. Add onions, cook until translucent and add garlic and jalapeño. Sauté until onions start to brown; add tomatillos and apples. Fill with stock and simmer 30 minutes. Add cilantro and bring to a boil. Blend to finish sauce. Add boiled heavy cream to base; season with salt and pepper. Finish with apple jack and simmer for 10 minutes. Add a little soft butter and blend, then pass through a fine chinois (or cheesecloth).

CONFIT OF DUCK

Serves 6 main courses or 12 salad portions

4 tbsp. salt
2 tbsp. chopped shallots
2 tbsp. lemon thyme
2 tbsp. cracked white peppercorns
1 bay leaf, crumbled
2 tsp. minced garlic
1 entire pod of garlic, cracked and peeled
1 tsp. mustard seeds
2 oz. vodka with peppers (Absolut is one brand)
8 to 10 duck legs, with thigh meat
4 1/2 cups duck fat, rendered

Combine all the above ingredients except duck legs and duck fat. Toss well in a bowl. Add duck pieces and rub the mixture into the flesh well. Cover the bowl with plastic wrap and refrigerate for 24 hours. Remove bowl; place duck into a clean bowl (reserve garlic from marinade for use later). Re-wrap and refrigerate for 6 more hours.

Heat the rendered duck fat to 200 degrees. Remove the duck meat from the bowl, dry with a paper towel, and slip into hot fat. Remove the garlic cloves from the marinade and add it to the fat; cover and cook in 200-degree oven until tender (approximately 2 1/2 hours). Test the meat with a wooden pick, which should go into meat with ease. Remove from oven and cool.

GORGONZOLA POLENTA

Serves 12

2 cups water
1 clove garlic, minced
1 cup yellow cornmeal
1 whole egg
1 egg yolk
2 tsp. Asiago, grated
1/3 cup Gorgonzola, crumbled
2 tsp. fresh basil, chopped
1 tsp. fresh thyme
1/2 tsp. salt
1 tsp. ground white pepper
1/4 cup white bread crumbs

In a heavy saucepan, bring water and minced garlic to a rapid boil. Quickly whisk in cornmeal. Lower heat to medium/low and stir constantly with a wooden spoon for 20 minutes (mixture should be very stiff). Remove mixture from heat and gradually stir in egg and egg yolk. Return pan to low heat and cook, stirring constantly, for 5 minutes. Add Asiago, Gorgonzola, basil and thyme, stirring to melt cheeses. Season to taste with salt and pepper.

Grease and lightly dust molds* with bread crumbs. Pipe or spoon polenta mixture evenly into molds. Set in a water bath. Cover lightly with greased wax paper or parchment paper and bake in center of oven at 325 degrees for 1 hour and 10 minutes. Allow to cool completely before unmolding.

---

* 12 one-inch stainless molds or one 10-inch Teflon cake pan, greased

SPINACH MOUSSE

12 portions

1 lb. fresh spinach, cleaned, stems removed
1 1/2 cups heavy cream
4 egg yolks
1/2 cup grated Asiago cheese
1 tsp. ground nutmeg
1/2 tsp. salt
1/2 tsp. ground white pepper

Blanch spinach in boiling, salted water. Remove to an ice bath and cool quickly. Drain and squeeze well to remove as much moisture as possible. Roughly chop spinach.

Place spinach along with all other ingredients in a blender and blend on high speed until smooth, about 30 seconds.

Grease timbals (or other molds)* and pour mixture in. Set molds in a water bath and bake, covered lightly with waxed paper, at 325 degrees for 40 minutes or until centers are firm to the touch. Remove from water bath and cool completely before unmolding.

---

* Fill 12 one-inch oyster cups of stainless steel, or one Teflon, 10-inch cake pan (greased), or use ramekins

ACTUELLE FRUIT COBBLER

Serves 8

Batter

1 cup cake flour, sifted
3/4 tsp. baking powder
1 cup sugar
2 whole eggs
6 oz. milk
1 tsp. vanilla
1 tsp. grated lemon or orange rind

Sift flour and baking powder. Add sugar, eggs, milk, vanilla, and zest. Mix well. Rest 1 hour in refrigerator before use.

Fruit for cobbler

1 apple
1 pear
2 oranges
1/2 pineapple
1/2 mango
1 banana
1/2 punnet raspberries
1 tbsp. brown sugar
1/2 tbsp. cinnamon
1/2 tbsp. maple syrup
1 tbsp. Grand Marnier

Clean, peel, and core fruit. Cut into medium dice, except berries. Toss fruit with brown sugar, cinnamon, maple syrup, and Grand Marnier. Marinate for several hours.

Preparation: Grease a shallow, 10-inch fireproof dish with a little butter. Dust with sugar. Place marinated fruit in dish. Pour 2 1/2 inches of batter over the fruit (use plenty of fruit). Bake in 350-degree oven for 25 minutes. Remove from oven and dust with powdered sugar.

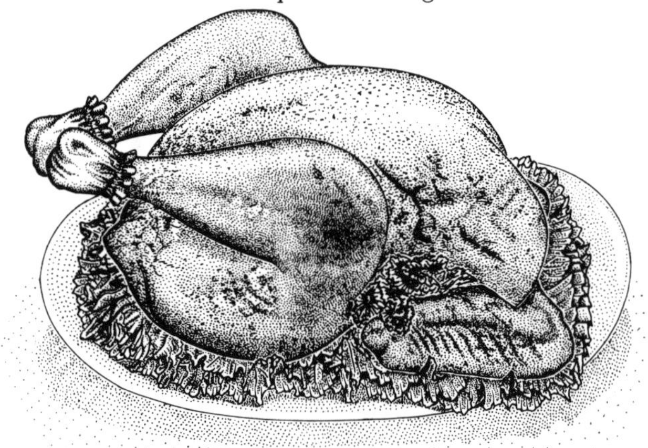

Anne Lindsay Greer

Born July 8, 1940, in Texas, Anne Lindsay Greer is a self-taught chef who has received the Tastemaker Award, "Who's Who in Food and Wine in Texas," and Who's Who in America. Chef Greer is credited by many as the instigator of Southwestern cuisine.

She says her most esteemed honors include recognition and respect from colleagues, being included in the first book about American chefs who influenced American cuisine, and being asked to write about the new Southwestern cuisine for *Gourmet* magazine.

She likes to cook risottos, anything grilled or cooked outdoors, and new combinations that use native ingredients and regional concepts that reflect the Southwest. When it comes to eating, give her biscuits, barbecue, and Mexican food. Greer's most embarrassing moment occurred on a PBS filming when she lost her voice from inhaling the fumes of jalapeño peppers.

Her best culinary moments include many, she says, but the very best ones have recognized the importance, validity, and good taste of Southwest cooking. As for her most fun event, it was cooking at the 1986 Napa Valley Wine Auction for Beringer Winery.

Aphorisms of Anne Lindsay Greer

1. There are no shortcuts to quality, whether frying chicken or making strawberry shortcake.
2. Have fun, be positive, and do what you love in work or any aspect of life.

CHEF ANNE LINDSAY GREER
6805 Midcrest
Dallas
(214) 239-3033

Menu

Spicy Crab and Dallas Cheesecakes
with Mango Cream and Red Pepper Cream
Buena Vista Fumé Blanc or Jordan Chardonnay

Chilled Green Chile Soup with Smoked Shrimp Salsa
Grand Cru Gewurztraminer or Alexander Valley Chenin Blanc

Tijuana Caesar Salad
Château Souverain Sauvignon Blanc or Inglenook Gravion

Grilled Wild Turkey with Cranberry Salsa
Acacia Pinot Noir or Cain Cabernet Sauvignon

Fresh Berry Brulee
Coffee
Gloria Ferrer Brut

SPICY CRAB AND DALLAS CHEESECAKES WITH MANGO CREAM AND RED PEPPER CREAM

Serves 6

Mango cream

1 large, ripe mango, peeled and chopped
1 cup creme fraiche (see following recipe for Green Chile Soup)
$^1/_2$–$^3/_4$ cup chicken stock
1$^1/_2$ tbsp. lime juice
Salt and pepper to taste

Put the mango in a blender jar and add the creme fraiche. Pulse the blender a few times, then blend as smooth as possible. Remove the center from the top, and with the blender running, add enough chicken stock to make a medium thick sauce, slightly coats spoon. Season with lime juice and salt and pepper to taste. Chill.

Red pepper cream

2 red bell peppers, roasted, peeled, seeded, stemmed, and cut up
2 tbsp. tomato paste (for color)
2 tbsp. warm vegetable oil, room temperature
1 clove garlic, chopped
1 cup creme fraiche
$^1/_2$–1 cup chicken stock
1 tbsp. lemon juice
Salt and pepper to taste

Put the red bell peppers and tomato paste in a blender jar. Add the warm oil, garlic, and $^1/_2$ cup of the creme fraiche. Blend a few seconds, then add the rest of the creme fraiche and enough chicken stock to blend smooth. The consistency should be the same as the Mango Cream. Add additional chicken stock if necessary. Season with lemon juice and salt and pepper. Chill.

Crab cheesecakes

2 tbsp. butter
1 clove garlic, minced
1 shallot, minced
3 tbsp. onion, minced
1 serrano chile, minced (do not seed)
$^1/_2$ lb. fresh crabmeat, bones and cartilage removed
$^1/_3$ lb. fresh goat cheeze (Mozzarella Company)
1 tbsp. fresh cilantro, minced
Salt and pepper to taste
$^1/_2$ cup cornbread crumbs
$^1/_2$ cup soft, fresh bread crumbs (French or Sourdough)
$^1/_4$ cup toasted pine nuts, chopped
Melted butter

Heat the butter in a small skillet over medium heat. Add the garlic, shallot, and onion and sauté a few minutes or until soft. Stir in serrano chile and set aside.

Combine the onion mixture with the fresh crabmeat, goat cheese and cilantro. Season to taste with salt and pepper.

Combine the cornbread crumbs, bread crumbs, and pine nuts and then toss with enough melted butter to moisten. Spread on a cookie sheet and toast in a 350-degree oven until golden brown, about 10–12 minutes. Set aside.

Form the crabmeat mixture into round cakes and then roll in the toasted crumbs. Heat in a 350-degree oven just long enough to warm, about 10–12 minutes.

TO SERVE:
Spoon about 2 oz. of each sauce on an appetizer plate. Place the crabcakes in the center and garnish with fresh cilantro leaves.

CHILLED GREEN CHILE SOUP WITH SMOKED SHRIMP SALSA

Serves 6–8

Salsa

1/2 lb. smoked shrimp (22–25 count), chopped
1/2 lb. small bay scallops, poached and chilled
2 shallots, minced
2 tbsp. each, red, yellow peppers, roasted, peeled, diced
1/4 cup mango, diced 1/4 inch
1 tbsp. red wine vinegar
1 tbsp. olive oil
1 tsp. each, cilantro and mint, chopped
Salt and pepper to taste
Fresh cilantro leaves

In a glass bowl combine the shrimp, scallops, shallots, peppers, and mango. Gently mix in vinegar, olive oil, and seasonings. Chill until ready to serve (may be made 12 hours in advance).

Soup

2 1/2–3 cups chicken broth
2 leeks, white part only
4 poblano chiles, roasted, peeled, stemmed, seeded
1 clove garlic, peeled
3 tomatillos, rinsed, husks removed and chopped
2 cups creme fraiche (recipe follows)
1 ripe avocado, peeled and stone removed
Salt and pepper to taste

Put the chicken broth and leeks in a saucepan over medium-high heat. Bring to a boil and allow to boil for 10 minutes. Strain.

Put the chiles, garlic, tomatillos, and half the creme fraiche in a blender jar. Blend on high speed about 2 minutes or until smooth. Add the avocado, and with the blender running, pour half the chicken broth through the top. Add remaining creme fraiche and blend smooth. Add enough additional chicken broth to make a medium thick soup. Season to taste with salt and pepper.

Creme fraiche

2 cups whipping cream
1/4 cup buttermilk
2 cups sour cream
Salt and pepper to taste

In a glass bowl stir together the heavy cream, buttermilk, and sour cream. Let stand at room temperature (about 75–80 degrees) for 2 hours. Stir and season to taste with salt and pepper and refrigerate until ready to use.

TO SERVE:
Ladle soup into shallow, wide soup bowls. Spoon the salsa in the center. Garnish with cilantro leaves and serve with strips of blue or yellow tortillas, fried crisp.

TIJUANA CAESAR SALAD

Caesar Salad was invented in Tijuana, Mexico, and remains one of my favorite salads. You can add grilled chicken to make an entrée salad, or smoked salmon.

Serves 4

Dressing

2 anchovies
1 clove garlic
1 small serrano chile, seeds and veins removed
1 egg
1/2 cup balsamic vinegar
1 tbsp. Worcestershire Sauce
2 tsp. Dijon or grainy mustard
1 cup light virgin olive oil
2 tbsp. fresh grated Parmesan cheese
Salt and pepper to taste

Salad

3 heads romaine lettuce leaves (use only the smaller, inner leaves)
1 large red bell pepper, roasted, peeled, and cut in strips
3 tbsp. pumpkin seeds, buttered and toasted
1½ cups croutons (see note)
½ cup Cotija cheese (Mexican dry crumbly cheese)
¾ cup Parmesan cheese, in shreds

In a blender or food processor combine all the dressing ingredients and blend until smooth. Set aside.

At service, toss the chilled lettuce leaves with peppers, croutons, pumpkin seeds, the dressing, and Cotija cheese. Divide among serving plates and garnish with shreds of Parmesan.

Note: To make croutons, toss large cubes of bread with coarse salt, pepper, olive oil, and cayenne pepper. (Be sparing with the cayenne.) Toast in a 350-degree oven until crisp.

GRILLED WILD TURKEY WITH CRANBERRY SALSA

This technique for wild turkey was a great success at Fall Creek Winery. Serve wild rice with pecans and wild mushrooms or wild rice cakes and fresh cornbread. Restaurant cooks may like to smoke additional parts to make a smoked sauce of natural juices, but it is not necessary as the turkey will be very juicy.

Cranberry salsa

1 red delicious apple, cored, unpeeled, and diced
Balsamic vinegar
1 pt. fresh raspberries
1 seedless orange, sectioned and chopped
1 cup sugar
1 pkg. (12 oz.) cranberries, coarsely chopped
Cassis or Blackberry brandy (optional)

In a glass bowl combine the apple with vinegar to retard browning. Add the raspberries, orange, sugar, and cranberries. Let stand for 1–2 hours. If desired, stir in 2 oz. of Cassis or Blackberry brandy.

Turkey and marinade

1–2 wild turkeys, cleaned, quartered (depending on size)
5 garlic cloves, crushed
3 sprigs fresh thyme
3 sprigs fresh rosemary
3–4 sprigs fresh basil
2 cups olive oil
½ cup balsamic vinegar
Juice from 2 lemons
1 tbsp. coarse ground pepper
1 cup chicken broth
1 small onion, minced
Sea salt
Coarse pepper

Combine the marinade ingredients and pour into a plastic bag. Marinate the turkey 3–4 hours, turning several times.

Prepare a large grill (preferably a kettle grill) using a combination of charcoal briquettes and mesquite wood charcoal. Burn the fire down until an ash begins to cover the coals. Spread the hot coals apart, so you have a fire at both sides. Soak wood chips in water.

Remove the turkey from the marinade, then salt and pepper all sides. Brown on both sides over the coals, grilling 10–15 minutes. Baste frequently.

Add the soaked, drained chips to the fire. Place the turkey, bone side down, in the center of grill, and, basting occasionally, cook an additional 45 minutes to 1 hour.

Remove from heat and let stand on warm platter, covered, for 10 minutes.

TO SERVE:
Slice meat from the breast and portions of dark meat, and serve with Salsa, wild rice, and cornbread.

Note: The key is to first brown the meat well, then cook over lower heat until tender.

FRESH BERRY BRULEE

Serves 8

Brulee

14 egg yolks
¾ cup sugar
Pinch salt
2 qts. whipping cream
6 oz. white chocolate, broken in several pieces
2 tbsp. vanilla extract

Berries

1 pt. fresh raspberries
1 pt. fresh blueberries
1 pt. fresh blackberries

Topping

1/2 cup brown sugar
1/2 cup granulated sugar
Fresh mint sprigs

In a medium bowl, whisk together the egg yolks, sugar, and salt until thickened, about 2 minutes.

In a large saucepan, heat the cream with the chocolate to a boil. Stir to melt the chocolate. Whisk 2 cups into the egg yolk mixture to warm the yolks.

Combine both mixtures in the saucepan, add vanilla, and continue to stir over medium heat for 5 minutes or until slightly thickened.

Pour the Brulee into a baking dish and bake in a water bath at 325–350 for 45 minutes or until soft set. Cool completely. Remove any skin from the top and then spoon the Brulee into a food processor and process until very smooth.

TO SERVE: Divide the berries in three mounds on 9- or 10-inch plates. Spoon or pipe (through a pastry bag) the mixture over the berries. Chill up to 4 hours.

Just before serving, mix together the two sugars and sprinkle over the Brulee, letting it spill onto the edges of the plate. Use a cook's propane torch and direct the flame to the sugar. Brown all the sugar, including that on the edge of the plate, until dark brown and caramelized. Serve immediately. Garnish with a mint sprig.

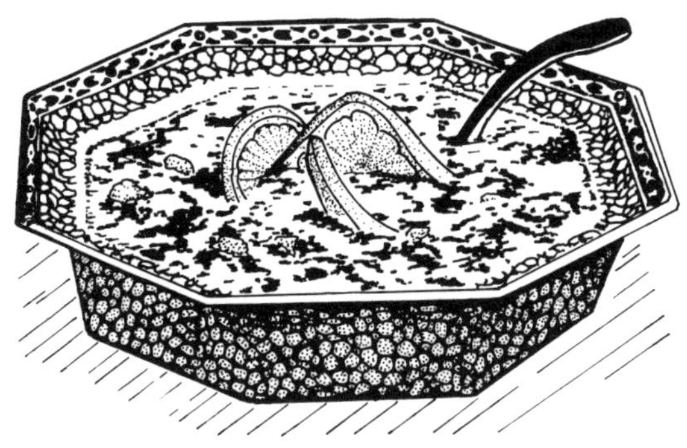

Lori Finkelman Holben

Lori Holben, born January 11, 1959, always wanted to be a blonde and named Donna. Among her favorite things are her mother's 1-2-3-4 birthday cake, shopping, celebrating her birthday, being awarded "Most Outstanding Student" at the Culinary Institute of America (CIA), graduating first in her CIA class, preparing salads, wearing Rockport shoes in the kitchen, eating hamburgers and French fries with ketchup, and hearing customers go "Mmmmm, this is wonderful" after tasting her food.

Her best tips to cooks are to use the food processor and to use salt and pepper.

David Holben

A native of Burlington, California, David Holben was born December 22, 1958. Among his favorite things are angel food cake, Thanksgiving, apprenticing in Roger Vergé's kitchen in France, being named a "Hot Chef of 1987" by *Food & Wine* magazine, wearing Rockports in the kitchen, preparing barbecue spareribs, eating spaghetti and meatballs, gardening, spoiling his two Siberian huskies, cooking for the American Institute of Food and Wine at La Hacienda Paloma Blanca in Mexico, and breakfast al fresco.

His most embarrassing culinary moment was to run out of a food item while preparing dinner for 100 people honoring Julia Child.

CHEFS LORI AND DAVID HOLBEN
The Riviera
7709 Inwood Road
Dallas
(214) 351-0094

Menu

Gnocchi Tart with Sausage, Peppers, and Mozzarella
Beringer Gamay Beaujolais or Chimney Rock Chardonnay

Maine Lobster and Gulf Crab Salad
with Grilled Belgian Endive and Tarragon
Slaughter-Leftwich Sauvignon Blanc or
Château Souverain Chardonnay

Red Snapper with Artichoke "Barigoule"
and Wild Rice Pancakes
Burgess Cellars Chardonnay or Château Souverain Zinfandel

Grilled Veal Medallions with Arugula
and Mushroom Butter Sauce
Benziger Merlot or Clos du Bois Cabernet Sauvignon

Creme Brulee

Coffee

Wimberley Valley Brut

GNOCCHI TART WITH SAUSAGE, PEPPERS, AND MOZZARELLA

10 small or 6 large tarts

6 cups milk
Dash salt and white pepper
13 oz. semolina
3 eggs
3 oz. or 3/4 cup parmesan cheese, grated
2 tbsp. olive oil
1 red bell pepper, roasted, peeled, and cut into strips
1 yellow bell pepper (same as red pepper)
1 small onion, thinly sliced and sautéed
3 oz. Moroccan olives, pitted
3 spicy sausages, cooked and cut in 1/8-inch rounds
1 lb. mozzarella cheese, grated
3 oz. romano cheese, grated
1 tbsp. fresh rosemary, finely chopped
Pinch of chili flakes

Tart bases:
Bring seasoned milk to a single boil. Add the semolina, stirring continuously and pressing out any lumps. Over medium heat, continue to cook about 15 minutes, stirring continuously. Transfer to a clean bowl and with an electric mixer beat in eggs and parmesan. Mix until well combined.

With wet hands, form into 6-inch rounds on an oiled sheet pan; pat smooth.

To assemble tarts:
Divide and arrange peppers, onion, olives, and sausage among the tart bases. Sprinkle mozzarella and romano cheeses on top; scatter rosemary and chili flakes over all. Bake tarts on well-oiled sheet pan for approximately 15 minutes at 375 degrees.

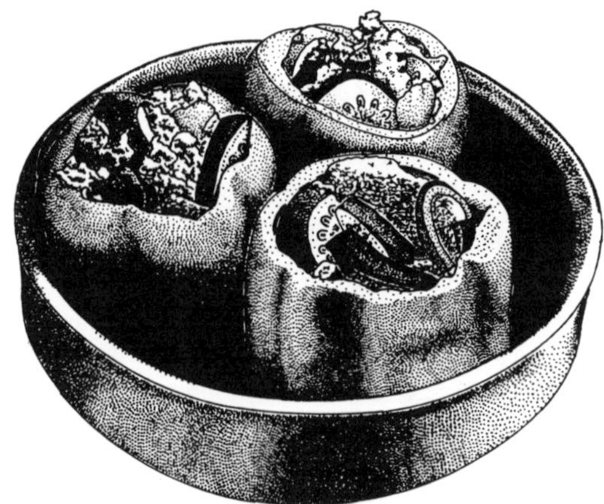

MAINE LOBSTER AND GULF CRAB SALAD WITH GRILLED BELGIAN ENDIVE AND TARRAGON

Serves 4

1 lemon
1/4 tsp. Dijon mustard
3 oz. extra virgin olive oil
4 heads Belgian endive
1/2 oz. extra virgin olive oil
1 (1 1/2-lb.) lobster, cooked, meat removed
6 oz. fresh lump crabmeat (shell particles removed)
2 small tomatoes, one red and one yellow, peeled, seeded, diced
Fresh tarragon leaves
Assorted baby lettuce leaves
Edible herb flowers (borage and sage work well)
Salt and white pepper

To prepare vinaigrette:
Grate the zest of half of the lemon into a bowl. Squeeze the juice from the lemon into the same bowl. Add the mustard and whisk. Add the olive oil; season with salt and pepper and reserve.

Split endive in half lengthwise. Brush with olive oil and season with salt and pepper. Grill endive over high heat until it is limp and slightly charred. Remove cores and julienne half of the endive.

Cut lobster meat into bite-size pieces. Mix with crab, tomatoes, tarragon, and endive julienne. Toss with all but 1 tbsp. of vinaigrette; season with salt and pepper.

Arrange grilled endive spears and lettuce leaves around the edge of each plate. Divide lobster and mix it among plates. Sprinkle herb flowers over top of salads.

RED SNAPPER WITH ARTICHOKE "BARIGOULE" AND WILD RICE PANCAKES

Serves 6

For artichokes:

3 artichokes
1 medium carrot, thinly sliced
1 small onion
2 tbsp. olive oil
2 oz. dry white wine
2 oz. chicken stock
Few rosemary sprigs

For pancakes:

4 oz. club soda
4 oz. heavy whipping cream
1 egg yolk
4 oz. flour
1/2 oz. butter, browned
1/2 cup fresh corn
1 cup cooked wild rice
1 tbsp. parsley
1/2 tsp. green peppercorns, crushed
Salt and white pepper to taste

For snapper:

6 (6-oz.) fresh red snapper filets, skinned and deboned
1 cup flour
3 oz. olive oil

For sauce (prepare just before serving):

4 oz. butter
1 1/2 oz. sun-dried tomato, julienned
12 blanched garlic cloves, sliced (to blanch, bring garlic cloves to a single boil in a little water in a saucepan; refresh in ice water; repeat one time, then peel)
2 oz. lemon juice
1 tbsp. chopped parsley

Artichoke preparation:

Pull or cut away the leaves of the artichokes, and trim each one down to the bottom or base. Scoop out the spiky choke and discard. Cut bottoms in 1/8-inch slices.

In a hot sauté pan, cook artichokes, carrots, and onion in olive oil. When beginning to soften, add white wine, chicken stock, and rosemary. Cook a few minutes longer, keeping vegetables *al dente*. Remove from heat and keep warm.

Pancake preparation:

Mix club soda, cream, and egg yolk in bowl. Stir in flour, add butter. Smooth out any lumps. Fold in corn, rice, parsley and peppercorns. Season with salt and pepper. Place spoonfuls of mix onto a hot griddle or sauté pan which has been lightly coated with oil. Flip pancakes when bubbly on top; remove and keep warm.

Snapper preparation:

Season fish filets and dredge in flour, shaking off excess. Sauté fish in a small amount of oil in a hot pan. Cook a few minutes until just translucent.

To serve:
Arrange artichokes on center of plate. Place fish on top and small pancakes around fish.

Prepare sauce when ready to serve. In a hot saucepan, melt butter until dark brown. Add remaining ingredients and pour over fish.

GRILLED VEAL MEDALLIONS WITH ARUGULA AND MUSHROOM BUTTER SAUCE

Serves 6

1 lb. white mushrooms
2 cups (1 lb.) unsalted butter, cut in small pieces
4 shallots, finely chopped
Few sprigs fresh thyme
1/2 cup chicken stock
1/2 cup dry white wine
Salt and white pepper
2 lbs. fresh veal medallions, cut from the loin or leg
1 tbsp. olive oil
3 cups packed arugula leaves, washed
1 tomato, peeled, seeded, diced

For sauce:
In a food processor, grind mushrooms until finely chopped. Melt 4 tbsp. butter in a saucepan; add shallots, mushrooms, and thyme. Cook over low heat, covered, just until mushrooms begin to release their juices, about 4 or 5 minutes.

Transfer mixture to a cheesecloth-lined strainer and let juices drain into a bowl, pressing down to release all liquid. Reserve mushroom mixture for another use.

In a stainless steel saucepan, combine mushroom juices, chicken stock, and white wine; reduce until thick and syrupy. Remove from heat and slowly whisk in remaining butter (1 1/2 cups), one piece at a time. Season with salt and pepper. Keep warm.

To serve:
Rub the veal with olive oil and season meat. Grill over a hot fire until medium rare (approximately 1 to 1 1/2 minutes each side).

Arrange arugula on plates; sprinkle tomatoes around perimeter of plates. Arrange veal in center of plates and drizzle with sauce.

CREME BRULEE

8 (4-oz.) servings

16 oz. heavy whipping cream
16 oz. half-and-half cream
6 oz. sugar
10 egg yolks
1 orange
3 oz. Grand Marnier
Dash of sugar

Bring cream and half-and-half to a single boil in a heavy stainless steel pot.

In a large mixing bowl, whip sugar and egg yolks until thick and lemony in color.

Temper hot cream by mixing with egg yolk mixture; return to pot. Cook over medium heat, stirring constantly. When mixture is thickened and coats the back of a spoon, remove from heat. (Do no let mixture boil.) Strain immediately into a chilled container and cool down the mixture.

Grate the zest of the cleaned orange into the mix. Add the Grand Marnier.

When cool, fill oven-proof ramekins with mixture. Place ramekins in water bath and bake at 350 degrees approximately 50 minutes or until custard is set. Refrigerate.

To serve, sprinkle sugar on top surface of custard. Place under the hot broiler until sugar is bubbly and slightly brulee (burned).

Timothy P. Keating

He calls himself a good Irish Catholic boy from the East Coast (born October 29, 1958, Passaic, New Jersey). If Timothy Keating had had any other name it would have been Jacques. However, he says, with such a name he would have forfeited his good Irish Catholic status.

"A cake I enjoy for birthdays is one baked by my good friend Jacques Torres of La Cirque in New York City called Gateau de la Grand Mere," he says. "It is a wonderful creation that his grandmother used to whip up on occasion. It's good for Christmas, too, my favorite celebration — not for all the gift giving, but for bringing my family (a mere ten children) together."

A fortune teller once told Chef Keating he had led very exciting lives in the past, some of them even risqué. "She also mentioned that I glowed with financial security as she handed me a bill for $25."

According to Chef Keating, his culinary training includes attending the University of Hard Knocks, "an education I hope never ends, because I believe experience is the best teacher of all."

His most esteemed honor was becoming executive chef at the Houston Ritz-Carlton after only one year with the company.

"I take great pride in working for this first-class, quality operation. It's a tightly bound family of ladies and gentlemen serving ladies and gentlemen."

His favorite things to cook include working with pasta, *foie gras,* lamb, softshell crabs, and wild game.

Chef Keating said his most embarrassing culinary moment was a culinary demonstration aboard John Wayne's boat, *The*

Spruce Goose, when he slammed head first (he is 6′8) into a lead pipe and knocked himself out cold. His best culinary moment was cooking for the 1988 Congress of the Chaine de la Rotisseurs at the Ritz-Carlton Rancho Mirage.

For relaxation he plays the guitar, plays golf, reads, and enjoys his friends.

His tip for cooks: "Technically speaking, I was taught that the way to peel tomatoes and garlic was to blanch them and then throw them in an ice bath to shock them; however, when in a big hurry, 10 seconds in the deep fryer and whoosh, no more skin."

Another one is to substitute white truffle powder from Oregon that "has a wonderful aroma and taste" in sauce Perigourdine instead of using whole black truffles.

Aphorisms of Timothy Keating

---

1. The most important ingredient in any recipe is care.
2. Set priorities in the workplace.
3. Take control of the tough problems and do not delegate them.
4. Set and demand standards.
5. Don't try to fix things that are impossible.
6. Be fair with employees but demand performance to the standards.
7. Everyone needs the ability to fail.
8. Nothing can be accomplished unless you're having fun.

CHEF TIM KEATING
Ritz-Carlton Hotel
1919 Briar Oaks
Houston
(713) 840-7600

Menu

Cold Papaya Soup, Blood Oranges,
Essensia wine, and Fresh Basil

Grand Cru Chenin Blanc or Mirassou Monterey Riesling

Raviolis of Rabbit and Tapioca,
Fennel and Mushrooms, and Pernod Cream

Freemark Abbey Johannisberg Riesling or Estancia Chardonnay

Tian of Smoked Salmon, Maine Lobster,
Caviar-Marigold-Mint Sauce

Grgich Hills Sauvignon Blanc or Slaughter-Leftwich Chardonnay

Black Buck Antelope Medallions, Cous Cous,
Poached Figs, and Texas Port Wine Sauce

Lyeth Red Table Wine or Rombauer Cabernet Sauvignon

Tart of Blueberries with Fresh Figs

Coffee

Domaine Mumm Napa Cuvee Brut

COLD PAPAYA SOUP, BLOOD ORANGES, ESSENSIA WINE, AND FRESH BASIL

Serves 2 as appetizer

1 medium-size ripe papaya
6 large basil leaves
1 each medium-sized blood orange
8 oz. essensia wine (California orange muscat, preferably 1985 vintage)
Raspberries to garnish
Opal basil top to garnish

Peel, split in half, and de-seed papaya. Cut halves in thin slices. Roll basil leaves into a cigar and slice very thinly to make chiffonade (shreds). Clean blood orange, removing all membranes; cut into clean sections (6 for each plate).

Arrange papaya on soup plate by gently laying down thin slices to make fan. Sprinkle each plate with chiffonade of basil. Arrange blood orange sections on each side. Pour essensia to just cover papaya. Garnish with a few raspberries and opal basil top.

Hint: Marinate fruit with wine on service plate a half hour before serving time to let flavors of all ingredients blend together.

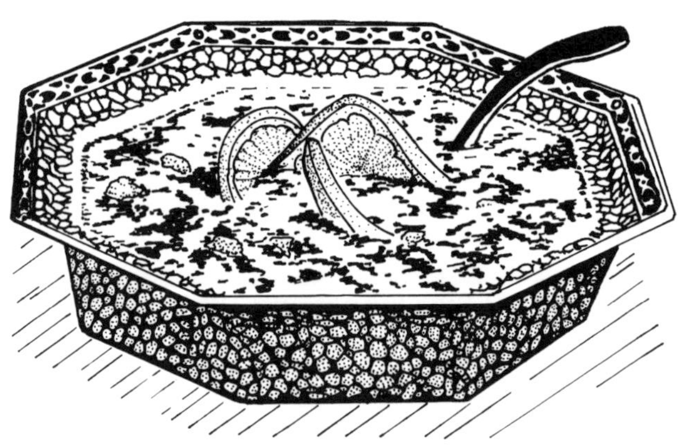

RAVIOLIS OF RABBIT AND TAPIOCA, FENNEL AND MUSHROOMS, AND PERNOD CREAM

Serves 6 as appetizer

1/2 lb. cleaned rabbit meat (reserving bones to prepare sauce)
3 oz. butter
8 oz. white wine
6 oz. rabbit stock
4 oz. Pernod
1 tsp. minced shallots
Salt and freshly ground white pepper
Pinch of chopped thyme or marjoram and tarragon (preferably fresh)
1 cup heavy cream
1/2 tsp. each minced chives and chervil
3 oz. tapioca
5 oz. milk (bring to boil, put in tapioca, cook about 8 minutes at simmer)
18 round Won Ton skins (or cut square wrappers with cookie cutter)
1/4 lb. select sliced shiitake, oyster, or hedgehog of morel mushrooms (if available)
1/4 cup slivered fennel
2 oz. diced tomatoes
1 sprig tarragon

In a hot skillet with 1 oz. butter, sauté rabbit pieces, stirring occasionally. De-glaze with 6 oz. white wine and stock, continuing to braise rabbit until tender. With slotted spoon, remove rabbit pieces; cool and dice finely. Continue cooking braising liquid until reduced by 1/4.

In a separate saucepan, brown rabbit bones, de-glaze with 3/4 Pernod, and flambé. Add shallots and reduce until 1 tbsp. Add remaining wine and herbs and reduce again. Add cream and gently boil until reduced by 1/2. Add strained liquid from rabbit braising and reduce until sauce coats the back of a spoon. Pass this through a fine strainer and return to fire. When it reaches a boil, whip in remaining butter and remaining Pernod. Sauce is ready to serve.

Ravioli filling:
Fold together diced rabbit, 1/2 of chives and chervil, and prepared tapioca seasoning. Form ravioli by placing a few teaspoons of filling in the center of each skin. Fold in 1/2 to form a crescent and then moisten edges and crimp closed. Poach in boiling salted water for 3 minutes. Remove with slotted spoon and drain well.

Sauté mushrooms, fennel, and remaining chives in 1/2 oz. butter until cooked but firm.

To serve:
Place mushroom mixture in center of plate, arranging ravioli in front and dressing with finished sauce. Sprinkle with confetti of diced tomatoes and tarragon bouquet.

TIAN* OF SMOKED SALMON, MAINE LOBSTER, CAVIAR-MARIGOLD-MINT SAUCE

Serves 2 as appetizer

1 each 1-lb. Maine lobster
1 tsp. Pasilla pepper (minced)
1 tsp. sweet yellow pepper (minced)
1 tsp. sweet red pepper (minced)
2 tsp. de-seeded diced tomatoes
1/2 tsp. chopped chives
1 tsp. mayonnaise
Juice of 1/2 small lemon
Salt and freshly ground pepper
Pinch of cayenne
3 oz. creme fraiche
4 sprigs of marigold mint (tarragon can be substituted)
1/2 tsp. each American sturgeon, golden and salmon caviars
1 oz. smoked Norwegian salmon
1/2 oz. rich lobster stock (optional for thinner sauce)

Pierce lobster through tail with wooden skewer (to keep tail straight for presentation purposes) and poach in boiling court bouillon for 7–8 minutes. Immediately cool in ice bath. Remove tail in one piece from shell and slice very thinly in medallions to garnish top of tian. Remove meat from elbows and claws of lobster; cut into cubes for mixing with peppers, 1/2 of tomatoes, chives, mayonnaise, 1/2 of lemon juice, seasonings. Toss all ingredients gently to coat evenly.

In a blender mix creme fraiche, marigold mint, remaining 1/2 of lemon juice, seasoning until well blended and smooth. Do not overmix. Gently fold in caviar.

Slice smoked salmon very thinly and cut into 3/4-inch x 5-inch strips to line small flan ring. Place ring on corner of 10″ plate. When lined with salmon, fill center with lobster mixture and top with lobster medallions arranged in pan on top of tian. Garnish with tomato dices and marigold mint sprig. Spread sauce around tian and serve chilled.

---

* Tian — shape of preparation

BLACK BUCK ANTELOPE MEDALLIONS, COUS COUS, POACHED FIGS, AND TEXAS PORT WINE SAUCE

Serves 2 entrées

6 (1 1/2-oz.) Texas black buck antelope medallions
2 each fresh figs
1 tbsp. honey
1/2 cup cous cous
1 cup chicken stock
1 tbsp. butter
1/4 tsp. salt
2 tsp. diced assorted bell peppers
Pinch of cayenne
1 each plum

Sauce:

1/2 lb. game bones (optional—antelope, venison, rabbit)
1 cup *mirepoix* (diced carrots, leeks, celery)
2 tsp. shallots
4 oz. Texas port wine
1 sprig thyme
1 sprig rosemary
1 sprig Italian parsley
6 oz. rich veal stock
1 oz. butter
1 tsp. black currant jelly

Sear antelope medallions in hot skillet until desired temperature (medium rare recommended) and remove from pan.

Poach figs for 4–5 minutes in port wine and honey and section in fourths for garnish.

Pour cous cous into 1 cup boiling chicken stock (game stock would be preferred if available). Add 1 tbsp. butter and 1/4 tsp. salt. Continue to boil for 2 minutes, stirring occasionally or until stock is almost absorbed. Remove from heat and cover tightly. Let stand for 10 to 15 minutes. Before presenting on plate, toss lightly with confetti of peppers and pinch of cayenne. Press cous cous mixture in small cup or mold and turn over on to center of plate.

For sauce:
If available chop game bones into small pieces and brown in saucepan with *mirepoix* and shallots. When browned, deglaze with 1/2 port. Add picked herbs and reduce to 1 tsp. Add remaining port and reduce again to 1 tbsp. Add veal stock and cook until reduced by 1/2. Pass through sieve or fine strainer and return to boil in saucepan. Remove from heat and whip in whole butter and 1 tsp. black currant jelly.

Arrange antelope around timbale of peppered cous cous, figs, and plums. Cover medallions with sauce and garnish plate with fresh herb bouquet.

TART OF BLUEBERRIES WITH FRESH FIGS

Yield: 4 round tarts

2 vanilla beans
3 cups whipping cream
10 egg yolks
6 oz. sugar
8 oz. puff pastry dough
4 oz. apricot jelly (for glazing)
4 fresh figs
8 oz. fresh blueberries

Steep split vanilla beans in whipping cream until just boiling. Remove from heat.

In mixing bowl, whisk egg yolks and sugar slowly over double boiler until creamy and light in texture. Slowly pour in the cream mixture until all is blended well. Remove from heat; pour into separate bowl and refrigerate well until ready to fill tart shell, along with blueberries to garnish.

Melt down apricot jelly to liquid and reserve to glaze finished tart.

Slice figs and layer on top of filled tart shell. Top with blueberries and paint with apricot glaze.

Serve with either freshly whipped cream or a fruit sauce made from fresh fruit puréed with a bit of confectioners sugar and passed through a strainer.

Joseph Mannke

Joseph Mannke was born in Kolberg, Pommerania, a state of Germany before World War II. He received his culinary training at the Hotel Bayerischer Hof in Munich. He loves chocolate in any form, including his birthday cake, and to sing all kinds of music. Chef Mannke's favorite things include Thanksgiving, awards from culinary shows, wearing boots in the kitchen, the Travel Holiday Magazine Award, eating seafood, preparing fresh vegetables and seafoods, and the Grand Restaurant Award from the *Wine Spectator*.

Culinary events are not always predictable, and Chef Mannke has had experience with the unexpected.

"My worst disaster actually wasn't my fault. I ordered 500 turkeys for my first Thanksgiving as chef at Disney World. I intended to stagger the delivery and told our supplier to split the order. Then I was surprised to receive 1,000 half turkeys!

"Another time, this time in Texas, I served small ice cream cones at intermission at a state dinner for French President Mitterand. With the Texas heat, the ice cream started to melt and dropped on his trousers. He had no choice but to lick his fingers. It was embarrassing for him, but also for me to see the French president embarrassed because of an American ice cream cone."

His best culinary moment was to open three hotels and thirty-three restaurants in 1971, serving 120,000 meals in one day during the opening of Walt Disney World. The most fun event, however, was to open his own restaurant.

He defines junk food as rich in calories and low in nutrition. "I stay away from it. I still have many plans for the future and need many more years to live to do it all."

His best substitute is margarine for butter.

Aphorisms of Joseph Mannke

1. Pay attention to details.
2. Shortcuts always mean trouble, and in most cases, it takes more time to fix things afterwards.
3. A chef is like a painter who combines colors to make a beautiful painting or a musician who combines notes and then makes a pleasant song. In each case it is the same: STAY WITH THE BASICS. Don't go way off the rocker with chocolate-covered ants or rattlesnake in fresh dill sauce.

CHEF JOE MANNKE

Rotisserie for Beef and Bird
2200 Wilcrest
Houston
(713) 977-9524

Menu

Swiss Onion Tart

Oberhellmann Semillon or Geyser Peak Soft Johannisberg Riesling

Roast Duck with Black Bing Cherries

The Hess Collection or Oberhellmann Cabernet Sauvignon or Pheasant Ridge Proprietors Reserve

Roast Rack of Lamb with Herbs and Garlic Crumbs

Llano Estacado Cabernet Sauvignon, Beringer Cabernet Sauvignon, or Buena Vista Cabernet Sauvignon

Breast of Pheasant with Fresh Mushrooms and Cognac

Duckhorn Merlot or Franciscan Cabernet Sauvignon

Fresh Raspberries with Zabaglione Sauce

Coffee

Domaine Montreaux Brut

SWISS ONION TART

Yield: 1 (9-inch) pie

1/4 stick butter
5 onions (thinly sliced)
1 tsp. salt
1/2 tsp. white pepper
1/2 tsp. whole thyme, chopped
4 slices lean bacon fried crisp (diced)
1 frozen 9 x 2-inch pie shell

Filling

1/4 cup flour
3 whole eggs
1 cup light cream
1 tsp. salt
Dash of fresh nutmeg

Heat the butter in a skillet; add the sliced onions and sauté until the onions are cooked, but not brown. Add salt, pepper, thyme, and crisp bacon.

Drain off the excess butter and pour the mixture into the pie shell.

For filling, sift the flour into a mixing bowl; add the eggs and beat well. Add the cream, salt, and nutmeg; combine all together and pour the mixture over the onions in the pie shell. Bake at 400 degrees for 25 minutes until golden brown and the egg and onion mixture is firm. Serve hot.

ROAST DUCK WITH BLACK BING CHERRIES

Serves 8

4 ducklings (2 lb. each)
4 tbsp. salt
2 tbsp. pepper
1 tbsp. rosemary
4 whole apples
1/2 cup soy sauce — double for more basting material
1/2 cup honey — double for more basting material

Season the insides of the ducklings with salt, pepper, rosemary, and the apples.

Secure the legs, wings, and neck skin to the body with cooking twine.

Place the duck breast up in the roasting pan, adding a little water, and roast for 1 hour and 30 minutes.

Baste with a mixture of soy sauce and honey every 10 minutes.

Sauce:

1 qt. brown gravy
1/2 cup burgundy
2 cups vinegar
1/2 lb. sugar
2 oranges, cut in pieces, peeled, membranes removed
1/2 cup orange marmalade
3 cloves
2 oz. Grand Marnier
1 cup bing cherries, pitted

Remove ducklings; tilt the roasting pan and drain all but a little fat. Add the brown gravy and burgundy and bring to a boil.

Bring vinegar in a heavy skillet to a boil; add sugar and reduce until sugar caramelizes to a golden brown color.

Dice oranges and combine with the browned sugar. Add orange marmalade and cloves and boil for 30 minutes. Strain and season with Grand Marnier and bing cherries.

ROAST RACK OF LAMB WITH HERBS AND GARLIC CRUMBS

Rack of spring lamb with 4 ribs
1 tbsp. salt
1/2 tbsp. each of fresh tarragon, chives, shallots, and parsley (all finely chopped)
1/2 cup bread crumbs
1 tsp. finely chopped parsley
2 cloves garlic (peeled and chopped)
1 tsp. mustard

Preheat oven to 450 degrees. Trim the fat from the ends of the chop bones by cutting down each rib bone about halfway toward the base, removing the rectangle of fat. The outside curve of the ribs has a thick crust of fat. Cut from the top, pull away this coating and discard.

Coat the meat all over with salt. Score the remaining fat and rub in the fine herbs on all surfaces. Roast at 450 degrees with fat side down for 15 minutes.

Combine the bread crumbs with the finely chopped parsley and garlic. Spread the mustard on the outside of the rack of lamb; top with the bread crumbs and return to the oven for 10–15 minutes. The bread crumbs should be nice and brown. Cut in chops and serve.

BREAST OF PHEASANT WITH FRESH MUSHROOMS AND COGNAC

Serves 6

3 pheasant breasts
4 tbsp. safflower oil
1 cup flour
2 tbsp. unsalted margarine
1 pt. fresh mushrooms (chopped)
1/2 onion (chopped)
3 tbsp. cognac
1 (10 1/2-oz.) can mushroom soup
1/2 cup pine nuts
1 cup green grapes

With a sharp knife, remove the skin from the pheasant breasts and discard. Cut along the breast bone and remove the breast. Cut into 2 pieces. Heat the safflower oil in a heavy skillet; dust the pheasant breast with flour and sauté over low heat on both sides until brown. Remove the pheasant from the pan and keep warm. Discard the oil.

In the same pan, melt the margarine and sauté the mushrooms and onions. Add cognac and the mushroom soup and bring to a boil. Spoon over the pheasant breast and serve.

Garnish with pine nuts and sliced green grapes.

FRESH RASPBERRIES WITH ZABAGLIONE SAUCE

Serves 6

3 pts. fresh raspberries (divide and place in 6 champagne glasses)

Sauce:

4 whole eggs
2 egg whites
1/2 cup sugar
1 cup dry Marsala wine
1/2 tsp. vanilla extract
Grated peel of 1/2 lemon (no white part)
6 sprigs of fresh mint

Place the first four sauce ingredients in the top of a double boiler and place over hot but not boiling water. Beat with a wire whisk, scraping the sides and bottom constantly until the mixture begins to foam up. Once the mixture is nice and creamy, add the vanilla extract and grated peel of lemon; combine well and spoon over the fresh raspberries.

Garnish with fresh mint and serve.

Robert McGrath

Born on March 8, 1954, in Louisville, Kentucky, Robert McGrath is a fun-loving free spirit. The evidence is in his answers to the biographical questions.

Q. What did you want to be named?
A. Ronald Reagan, or anyone with the last name of Kennedy, Rockefeller, or DuPont.
Q. What is your favorite birthday cake?
A. My 21st.
Q. Your favorite celebration?
A. Life!
Q. What was your culinary training?
A. Eyes and ears open — mouth shut!
Q. What shoes do you wear in the kitchen?
A. Sears Diehard (neck bolts optional).
Q. What have fortune tellers told you?
A. I'm a woman in a man's body. No, not really. I'm Richard Nixon.
Q. Awards and recognitions?
A. Yes, gold medals for food. [26 at last count — SJE]
Q. Most esteemed honor?
A. Named one of the best chefs in America by *Food & Wine;* also being the graduation speaker at the Culinary Institute of America.
Q. Favorite dish to cook?

A. At home, grilled kosher hen, sweet potato, silver queen corn.
Q. Favorite dish to eat?
A. Seafood — any kind.
Q. What's your worst culinary disaster?
A. Can't remember.
Q. Your most embarrassing culinary moment?
A. Crashing President Carter's dessert into a glass door.
Q. Your best culinary moment?
A. All of them.
Q. Most fun event?
A. "Evening with the Masters" — an annual event benefiting cystic fibrosis.
Q. Your most difficult preparation?
A. "Share Our Strength" dish. Nothing is really too difficult for us, yet everything is hard work.
Q. How do you spend your day off?
A. Different every time. Usually outdoors.
Q. Your favorite tip to cooks?
A. Don't get into cooking unless you love it.
Q. The best shortcut?
A. Taking Houston's 610 South instead of Highway 59. There are no shortcuts in cooking for doing things the best way.
Q. Most successful substitute?
A. None.
Q. What's your philosophy?
A. Have fun, high quality.
Q. Define junk food. Do you eat it?
A. Anything with ingredients that look like they came from NASA. Sometimes.
Q. Do you sing or whistle in the kitchen?
A. For music pleasure, I play the saxophone.

CHEF ROBERT McGRATH

The Deville in Houston's Four Seasons Hotel
1300 Lamar — Houston — (713) 650-1300

Menu

Smoked Lamb Nachos
Navarro Pinot Noir, Simi Chardonnay, or Sanchez Creek Chambourcin

Big Spring Rattlesnake and Toasted Pumpkin Seeds on Ancho Linguini with a Lime Cream
Clos Pegase Sauvignon Blanc or Robert Keenan Merlot

Mixed Field Greens with a Rosemary Vinaigrette
Quail Ridge Sauvignon Blanc or Sunny St. Helena Gewurztraminer

Bobwhite Quail Breast Wrapped in Veal Bacon on Black Pepper Cream
Beringer Chardonnay, Calera Pinot Noir, or A. Rafanelli Zinfandel

Charcoaled Axis Venison with Grilled Summer Vegetables and a Red Bell Pepper Sauce,
Lo-Cal Green Apple and Jicama Slaw, and
Sage Cornsticks
Haywood Cabernet Sauvignon, Beaulieu Cabernet Sauvignon, or Villa Mt. Eden Cabernet Sauvignon

Charcoaled Black Buck Antelope with Roasted Garlic Pasta and Tomato Chutney and Pinot Noir-Rosemary Glacé
Arrowood Cabernet Sauvignon, Laurel Glen Cabernet Sauvignon, or Dominus

Cobbler of Peaches, Basil, and Sour Cherries with a Southern Comfort Sauce
Coffee
Korbel Sparkling Brut

SMOKED LAMB NACHOS

Serves 4

8 oz. lamb tenderloin (smoked), chiapetti lamb
8 oz. poached tortilla chips
6 tbsp. refried black beans
6 tbsp. pico de gallo

Arrange these items vertically on the plate:

#1 #2 #3 #4

#1 — refried black beans
#2 — poached tortilla chips
#3 — sliced (smoked) lamb tenderloin
#4 — pico de gallo

Smoked lamb tenderloin

Season tenderloin with salt and pepper and grill (using mesquite wood) according to personal preference. Tenderloin can also be cooked in a cast-iron skillet or broiled. Keep covered until ready to use. Then slice and arrange according to diagram.

Poached tortilla chips

1/2 tsp. garlic, chopped fine
1 tsp. jalapeño, chopped fine
6 oz. tortilla chips, corn
3 oz. heavy cream
1 1/2 oz. grated Monterey Jack cheese

In a hot skillet place garlic and jalapeño to sweat. Quickly add tortilla chips and heavy cream; reduce by half. Finish with the grated Jack cheese. Keep warm until arranged on plate.

Refried black beans

1 lb. black turtle beans, soaked in water
1 bulb garlic, chopped coarse
1/2 gallon chicken stock
1/2 jalapeño, chopped fine
1/2 onion (small), diced

Soak the beans for 8–10 hours. Place in a colander to drain. Place all ingredients in a large pot and boil hard for 20 minutes; then a slow boil for 2–3 hours (you may need to add a little water as the beans cook).

Pico de gallo

3 (4 x 5) beefsteak tomatoes, diced
1 small onion, chopped
3–4 cloves garlic, minced
1 small jalapeño, chopped fine
1 small bunch cilantro, chopped
3 limes, squeezed for juice
1/2 jicama, peeled and chopped

Combine ingredients.

BIG SPRING RATTLESNAKE AND TOASTED PUMPKIN SEEDS ON ANCHO LINGUINI WITH A LIME CREAM

4 Servings

Ancho linguini

2 extra large eggs
1 egg yolk
1 1/2 cups dark chili powder
1 tbsp. paprika
1 tsp. cumin
1/2 tsp. cayenne
1 1/4–1 3/4 cups flour

Mix the ingredients in a mixer until pieces about the size of walnuts start breaking. Start with 1 cup flour and add more if consistency needs it. Do not overmix; the pasta should not be sticky to the touch. Cut the pasta into pieces approximately the size of a tennis ball, and flatten. Roll through a hand crank pasta machine (Atlas) to the #5 setting, then through the linguini cutter attachment. Cook in salted water with a little oil (olive or vegetable). Hold aside, covered.

Lime cream

1 oz. butter, clarified
2 shallots, chopped fine
4 cloves garlic, chopped fine
4 1/2 oz. dry white wine
2 limes, juiced and zested (reserve zests to finish sauce)
18 oz. heavy cream
Salt and pepper

In a hot skillet add the butter, shallots, and garlic (careful not to burn the garlic); cook quickly. Add white wine and reduce by half. Add the lime juice and reduce by one-third. Add the cream and reduce by one-third. Strain through a fine strainer. Finish with lime zests, and season with salt and pepper. Yield 12 oz.

Toasted pumpkin seeds

4 tsp. pumpkin seeds
1/2 tsp. salt
1/10 tsp. cayenne
1/4 tsp. cumin
1/4 tsp. chili powder
1/2 tsp. olive oil

Spread the pumpkin seeds on a sheet pan. Season and oil, then mix. Toast until crisp, approximately 8–10 minutes in a 350-degree oven.

Final preparation:

2 oz. vegetable oil
8 oz. rattlesnake filet, cut into fingers (4 x 2)
5 cloves garlic, chopped fine
2 shallots, chopped fine (optional)
8 oz. Ancho Linguini (4 x 2)
1 large red bell pepper, roasted, peeled, seeded, cut into matchsticks
1 large gold bell pepper, roasted, peeled, seeded, cut into matchsticks
2 med. poblano peppers, roasted, peeled, seeded, cut into matchsticks
2 oz. whole butter
12 oz. Lime Cream (4 x 3)
4 tbsp. Toasted Pumpkin Seeds

Heat a pot of salted water to slow boil. Warm Lime Cream sauce to 145 degrees. In a large skillet add oil. Heat to "smoking-hot"; add rattlesnake and keep it moving. Jump the snake in the skillet approximately 2 minutes; then add garlic and shallots. Remove from flame but keep warm. Heat a second skillet. Drop the pasta in the water and heat. Remove from water and put in skillet with the peppers; add whole butter and jump. Season with salt and pepper to taste.

Place 2 oz. of pasta per plate in the center; 3 oz. of sauce around permimeter; place 2 oz. of snake (small pieces) around perimeter on sauce; sprinkle 1 tbsp. of pumpkin seeds on the pasta.

MIXED FIELD GREENS WITH ROSEMARY VINAIGRETTE

4 Servings

1 head radicchio
2 heads frissee lettuce
6 heads mache greens
2 bunches watercress
2 bunches arugula

Wash and dry the greens and toss together.

Rosemary vinaigrette

1 cup fresh rosemary, chopped fine
1 cup rice vinegar, low acidity
2 tsp. white Worcestershire
3 each shallots, chopped
Juice from 1/2 lemon
1/4 cup corn oil
6 oz. Dallas Mozzarella
Tomato slices

Mix dressing; toss with field greens. Place slice of Dallas Mozzarella on peeled tomato slice and serve.

BOBWHITE QUAIL BREAST WRAPPED IN VEAL BACON ON BLACK PEPPER CREAM

12 Servings

12 quail breasts, seasoned with salt and pepper
6 slices veal bacon (recipe follows)
6 oz. black pepper cream (recipe follows)
12 oz. tomato flesh, julienne

Wrap 1/2 slice of veal bacon around quail breast and secure with a toothpick. Roast in 375-degree oven for 8 to 10 minutes. Remove the toothpick and place on sauce. Garnish with tomato julienne.

Veal bacon

1 veal breast, boneless
20 lbs. rock salt
2 lbs. brown sugar
20 gallons water
1 lb. sodium nitrite
12 bay leaves
2 oz. juniper berries
curing brine (this is the batch size, you do not need all of this for one veal breast)

Cover veal breast in brine for 12 hours, then smoke-roast at 175–180 degrees for 4–4 1/2 hours.

Black pepper cream

1 oz. butter, clarified
3 garlic cloves, minced
1/2 shallot, minced
4 oz. white wine
1 tbsp. cracked black pepper (level tbsp.)
12 oz. heavy cream

Heat butter in saucepan. Add shallots and garlic (careful not to burn garlic) and sweat them. Add wine and reduce by half. Add pepper while reducing wine. Add cream and reduce by half.

CHARCOALED AXIS VENISON WITH GRILLED SUMMER VEGETABLES AND A RED BELL PEPPER SAUCE

2 (2 1/2 to 3 oz.) medallions of Texas Axis Venison (per person)

Herb marinade (optional)

Add olive oil to just cover meat. Mix in with meat and oil: chopped parsley, thyme, rosemary, sage, garlic, basil. If time permits, marinate 2 days. Before charcoaling, wipe off excess oil. The remaining oil will cook off, so what you end up with is a nice flavoring from the herbs with no added calories.

Red bell pepper sauce

2 tbsp. cotton seed oil
1 clove garlic, chopped
4 shallots, chopped
4 red bell peppers (seeds and stems removed and peppers cubed)
6 tbsp. white wine
1 cup chicken stock
1/2 tsp. cayenne pepper
1/2 tsp. cumin
Salt
Freshly ground black pepper

Heat oil and sauté garlic and shallots for 1 minute at low heat. Add red peppers and sauté for 5 minutes until peppers begin to soften, but don't allow garlic and shallots to brown. Add white wine and chicken stock and bring to a boil. Season with cayenne pepper, cumin, salt, and black pepper. Simmer until red peppers are soft.

Carefully purée bell pepper mixture in blender until smooth and return to stove. Reduce purée until it reaches proper consistency. Serve on plate under meat.

LO-CAL GREEN APPLE AND JICAMA SLAW

Serves 4

3 (medium size) tart green apples
1 (medium size) jicama
1 (small) red bell pepper
1 tbsp. chopped parsley
3 tbsp. tarragon vinegar
6 tbsp. rice vinegar
3 tbsp. Texas marigold honey (optional)
Salt
Freshly ground white pepper

Peel, core, and cut apple into matchstick-size pieces. Peel and cut jicama into matchstick-size pieces. Roast, peel, and seed red pepper and cut into julienne.

Combine apple, jicama, bell pepper, parsley, vinegars, honey, salt and pepper. Toss until well mixed.

Serve cold and crispy with your favorite grilled entrée for a great hot weather accompaniment.

SAGE CORNSTICKS

Yield: approximately 30

5 oz. granulated sugar
1 lb. 5 oz. regular flour
11 oz. cornmeal
2 oz. baking powder
1 pinch salt
1/4 oz. sage
1 lb. 4 oz. milk
6 eggs
10 oz. oil

Method: First mix all dry ingredients, then add liquid ingredients slowly. Cook at 400 degrees, approximately 14 minutes in corn-shaped molds.

CHARCOALED BLACK BUCK ANTELOPE WITH ROASTED GARLIC PASTA AND TOMATO CHUTNEY AND PINOT NOIR-ROSEMARY GLACÉ

Serves 4–6

12 (3-oz.) black buck antelope loin, in medallions
1 pt. extra virgin olive oil
1 pt. Pinot Noir
6 cloves garlic, crushed
2 shallots, peeled and crushed
15 black peppercorns
1/2 jalapeño pepper, split
2 sprigs rosemary
2 oz. celery leaves

Make marinade from above ingredients and marinate the antelope for 8 hours. This product is very tender; the main objective is to impart additional flavor to complement the other accompaniments served with the antelope.

Roast garlic pasta

3 bulbs garlic (peeled, poached in milk 5–7 minutes, then roasted)
5 extra large eggs
1 tsp. salt
1 tbsp. black pepper
2 lbs. flour

Purée the garlic and mix with the eggs, salt, and pepper. Add flour and mix until dough falls off in the bowl. Roll out on a smooth, floured surface and cover. Cut into sections and roll through pasta machine and cut fettucine. Poach in salted, oiled water and hold.

Tomato Chutney

12 (5 x 5) tomatoes (peeled, seeded, and very coarse chop)
3 garlic cloves, minced
1 shallot, minced
1/2 onion, chopped
1 small jalapeño pepper, chopped
1 tbsp. ginger, chopped
1/4 bunch cilantro, chopped
7 oz. malt vinegar
4 oz. molasses
6 oz. brown sugar
1/2 tsp. salt

Mix ingredients.

Pinot Noir-Rosemary Glacé

1 lb. antelope, trimmings from the loin
1 carrot, chopped
1/2 onion, chopped
1 clove garlic, chopped
10 oz. Pinot Noir
32 oz. veal stock; beef can be substituted
1/2 tsp. black pepper
4 sprigs rosemary

Heat saucepan hot. Add the meat trimmings and vegetables except the garlic. Keep moving until meat is browned and vegetables are soft. Add garlic; do not burn it! As it begins to brown add 8 oz. of the wine and reduce by half. Add pepper and rosemary with stock and reduce by half. Strain and add 2 oz. wine.

The finished plate:
Nap the plate with 2 oz. of Pinot Noir-Rosemary Glacé. Toss 2 1/2 oz. of pasta in a very little butter (1 oz.). Place grilled medallions on plate next to pasta. Place good tablespoon of tomato chutney on antelope. Garnish plate with rosemary sprig, if desired.

COBBLER OF PEACHES, BASIL, AND SOUR CHERRIES WITH A SOUTHERN COMFORT SAUCE

Serves 6

Cornmeal crust

1 cup very fine cornmeal
1 1/2 cups all-purpose flour
3/4 cup sugar
1 tsp. salt
5 tsp. grated lemon peel
1 lb. butter
3 egg yolks
1 1/2 tsp. honey
1 1/2 tsp. vanilla

Blend dry ingredients, including lemon rind. Cut cold butter in small pieces into the mix. Process it until it is very coarse.

Mix well the yolks, honey, and vanilla. Blend into dry mixture until it comes together. Separate portions and refrigerate for a couple of hours.

Roll between parchment paper and dust with masa harina for easier handling. Bring to desired thickness and cover previously buttered and floured pans. Reserve leftover dough.

Peach and cherry filling

2 lbs. seeded, unpeeled, ripe peaches
12 oz. black cherries, pitted
1 leaf basil, torn
1 tbsp. lemon juice
2 tbsp. masa harina
1 tbsp. sugar

Cut peaches into 1/4-inch wedges and toss with cherries and basil in lemon juice. Sprinkle sugar and the masa harina on top and distribute evenly.

Fill shells. Arrange to fit pattern.

Roll some leftover dough into strips and bake until golden brown. Let cool; crumble and mix with fruit. Roll remaining dough into strips and place on top. Bake at 350 degrees for 10 minutes. Lower to 300 and bake until golden brown.

Bourbon vanilla sauce

1 qt. half-and-half
1 vanilla bean, split
7 egg yolks
4 oz. sugar
1/3 cup Southern Comfort

Scald the half-and-half with the vanilla bean. Meanwhile, beat the yolks and sugar to a ribbon. Strain the milk and remove vanilla bean.

Temper the yolks with half-and-half, then stir the rest of the milk briskly into the mixture. Pour the entire mixture into a clean pot and heat on low until sauce covers the back of a spoon. Remove and place over ice until cooled down. Add Southern Comfort and refrigerate.

Bruce Molzan

Bruce Molzan, born February 20, 1958, in Virginia, agrees with half the top toques who prefer some sort of chocolate cake for their birthdays. He has never gone to a fortune teller, and he shares the enthusiasm of several chefs who say Christmas is their favorite celebration.

He attended the Culinary Institute of America for his culinary training, and his most esteemed honor was cooking for Chris Evert before she won the Virginia Slims tennis tournament in Houston.

Day fresh fish is Chef Molzan's favorite dish to cook and to eat, but with cheese ravioli, pesto, and arugula. When asked about his worst disaster, he replied, "I was preparing for a lavish dinner party for twelve and I had exactly enough — but no more — of the *foie gras*. My wife, thinking there was an extra portion, ate one. My most embarrassing moment was telling the host that my wife had eaten his *foie gras*."

Chef Molzan says pastries are the most difficult to make.

His philosophy is to cook food the way he likes to eat it and serve it in the atmosphere he most enjoys — a casual and fun environment.

Aphorisms of Bruce Molzan

1. Don't be a slave to a recipe; experiment with what you have and what you like.
2. There are no shortcuts or substitutions when it comes to fine cuisine.

CHEF BRUCE MOLZAN

Ruggles Grill
903 Westheimer
Houston
(713) 524-3839

Menu

Crispy Shrimp Salad with Avocado Vinaigrette

Hacienda Sauvignon Blanc or Chalone Pinot Blanc

Snapper Baked in Herb Crust with
Summer Crawfish Vinaigrette

Silver Oak Cabernet Sauvignon Alexander Valley or Caymus Cabernet Sauvignon

Corn Chowder with Fresh Crab and Avocado

Clos Pegase Chardonnay or Caymus Sauvignon Blanc

Grilled Chicken with Ancho Chili Cream

Stemmler Pinot Noir or Geyser Peak Merlot

Ruggles' Chocolate Parfait

Coffee

Jepson Brut

CRISPY SHRIMP SALAD WITH AVOCADO VINAIGRETTE

Serves 6

2 ears fresh corn
2 large Idaho potatoes
18 shrimp, peeled and deveined
Flour for dredging
2 eggs, beaten
2 tbsp. olive oil
1 head Boston lettuce
1 head red leaf lettuce
1 bunch spinach
1 head romaine
12 arugula leaves (6 for garnish)
1 endive, julienned
1 pt. cherry tomatoes, halved
6 lemon wedges for garnish

Roast corn in the husks for approximately 10 minutes in a 400-degree oven. When cooled, peel away husks, cut kernels from cob, and reserve. Shred one Idaho potato in processor or with potato shredder; boil, peel, and cube the other.

Dip shrimp to coat in flour, then egg, then shredded potato. Sauté in large skillet in olive oil till crisp and brown. While shrimp are sautéing, prepare greens for salad.

Combine greens with corn, cubed potato, and cherry tomatoes and toss with Avocado Vinaigrette (recipe follows).

Avocado vinaigrette

1 avocado
2 tbsp. Dijon mustard
1 clove garlic
1 jalapeño, seeded
2 shallots, peeled
Juice from 4 limes
1/3 cup champagne vinegar
2 tbsp. fresh chopped cilantro
1 tsp. fresh basil
Salt and freshly ground pepper to taste
2 tsp. honey
1 cup (approximately) olive oil

Put all ingredients except olive oil in blender or food processor. Purée and add oil slowly until mixture is thick and congealed. May take more or less oil.

To assemble:
Place generous serving of tossed salad on each chilled plate. Lay 3 sautéed shrimp on side and garnish with arugula leaf and lemon wedge.

SNAPPER BAKED IN HERB CRUST WITH SUMMER CRAWFISH VINAIGRETTE

Serves 6

6 fresh filets of red snapper
1/4 cup olive oil
Basil leaves for garnish

Herb crust

1/2 baguette fresh French bread, cubed
2 strips cooked bacon
2 tbsp. fresh basil
2 tbsp. fresh chives
2 tbsp. fresh parsley

Pulse in food processor till mixture forms crumbs.

Summer crawfish vinaigrette

3 tbsp. olive oil
2 tbsp. butter
1 shallot, peeled and finely chopped
2 tbsp. chopped red onion
5 Greek black olives, pitted and chopped
1 cucumber, peeled, seeded and chopped
2 tbsp. chopped fresh red pepper
2 tbsp. chopped fresh yellow pepper
1 tbsp. fresh chopped basil
Juice of 2 lemons
Salt and pepper to taste
1/2 cup cooked crawfish tails

In a large skillet, over medium-high heat, melt butter with olive oil until sizzling. Add shallots and red onion and sauté about 1 minute. Add other ingredients one by one, stirring and sautéing briefly to combine.

Dip snapper filets in olive oil then dredge in seasoned bread crumbs (Herb Crust). Place in oiled baking pan and bake in 400-degree oven approximately 10 minutes.

To assemble:
Pour Crawfish Vinaigrette on plate and place filet on top. Garnish with fresh basil leaves.

CORN CHOWDER WITH FRESH CRAB AND AVOCADO

Serves 6

10 ears fresh corn
1 stick butter, melted
1 1/2 onions, peeled and chopped
2 stalks celery, chopped
1/2 red pepper, seeded and chopped
1/2 yellow pepper, seeded and chopped
1 small poblano, seeded and chopped
1 qt. intense chicken stock
1 qt. whipping cream
Salt and freshly ground pepper to taste
1 lb. jumbo lump crab
1 avocado, chopped
Roasted Poblano Purée (recipe follows)
Cilantro for garnish

Shuck corn and cut off kernels. Melt butter in large saucepan. Sauté corn, onions, celery, red pepper, yellow pepper, and poblano for about 8 to 10 minutes. Add chicken stock and reduce uncovered at a brisk simmer for about 30 minutes. Add cream, salt and pepper, and continue to reduce for another 30 minutes. Pour into food processor and purée. Strain.

Place about 1 tbsp. of crabmeat and 1 tsp. avocado into each soup bowl. Pour hot soup on top and drizzle poblano purée on top. Garnish with sprigs of cilantro.

Roasted poblano purée
Oil 5 fresh poblanos and broil in oven until blackened and blistered on all sides. Place in plastic bag in freezer for 10 minutes. Remove and, under running water, peel away skin and remove seeds. Purée in blender and strain.

GRILLED CHICKEN WITH ANCHO CHILI CREAM

Serves 6

6 chicken breast halves
6 shiitaki mushrooms
6 thick slices onion
2 tbsp. butter
2 cloves garlic
1 shallot, peeled and chopped
1 tbsp. honey
Ancho Chile Paste (recipe follows)
1/2 cup Beurre Blanc (recipe follows)
Spicy Salsa (recipe follows)
6 tbsp. sour cream

Grill chicken breasts with mushrooms and onion slices over hot coals, approximately 5–6 minutes.

Sauté garlic and shallots in butter quickly. Add honey and Ancho Chile paste. Allow to bubble about 1 minute. Take off heat and add 1/2 cup Beurre Blanc. Take care not to boil. Season with salt and freshly ground black pepper.

To assemble:
Place sauce on bottom of plate. Put chicken breast with mushroom and onion slice on top of sauce. Garnish with heaping tablespoon Spicy Salsa and sour cream.

Spicy salsa

3 large tomatoes, peeled, seeded, and chopped
3 large shallots, peeled, seeded, and chopped
2 cloves garlic, chopped
1 1/2 jalapeños, seeded and chopped
4 tbsp. olive oil
Salt and freshly ground black pepper to taste
2 tbsp. chopped cilantro
Juice of 1 lime

Beurre blanc

4 tsp. finely chopped shallots
3 cups vermouth
Juice of 4 lemons
1 tbsp. champagne vinegar
2 cups cream
1 lb. butter
Salt and freshly ground pepper to taste

In a medium-sized saucepan, combine shallots, vermouth, lemon juice, and vinegar. Reduce over low heat to about 1/4 cup. Add cream and continue reducing over low heat until reduced by half. Whip in butter tablespoon by tablespoon. Season with salt and pepper to taste.

Ancho chile paste

6 ancho chiles
2 white onions
1 head garlic
1/2 cup honey
3/4 cup wine vinegar
2 cinnamon sticks (whole)
7 whole cloves
1/4 cup toasted pine nuts
1 tsp. black peppercorns
Salt to taste

Rinse chiles under water to clean; wipe dry. Be careful not to crack open chiles. Place dry sauté pan over moderately high heat. One by one, sear each chile in hot pan until skin puffs and crackles, about 10 seconds each side. Use spatula to press chile against hot pan.

As you remove chiles from pan, place them in bowl of hot water. When all the chiles are in the bowl, place a small plate on top of them to keep them submerged in the water. Soak for 30 minutes. Remove from water and discard the stem and set peppers aside. To reduce the "heat" of these hot peppers, remove the seeds at this point.

Cut onion and garlic heads in half and, leaving skins on, place skin side down over hot grill. Roast until onion and garlic are soft and cooked through, about 30 minutes. Don't burn. Remove and set aside when done. When cool, peel off skins.

Place honey, vinegar, cinnamon sticks, cloves, pine nuts, and black peppercorns in blender. Process until spices are ground. Add garlic, onions, and chiles. Continue to blend until smooth. Add 1/2 tablespoon salt or to taste.

Note: Can be used as marinade for roasted or grilled meats and fish.

RUGGLES' CHOCOLATE PARFAIT

Chef/owner Bruce Molzan got inspiration for this layered, chocolate-on-chocolate dessert on a trip to Paris, where he worked in the kitchens of some of its most celebrated restaurants. "This is my absolute favorite chocolate dessert," says the CIA honors graduate.

Serves 4

Chocolate cake

1 cup cocoa
2 3/4 cups all-purpose flour
2 tsp. baking soda
1/2 tsp. salt
1/2 tsp. baking powder
1 cup butter
2 1/2 cups granulated sugar
4 eggs
1 1/2 tsp. vanilla
2 cups water

Preheat oven to 350 degrees. In a mixing bowl, sift together the cocoa, flour, baking soda, salt, and baking powder.

In a separate bowl, using an electric mixer, cream the butter with the sugar, eggs, and vanilla.

Combine the two mixtures alternately in a third bowl, adding the water. Pour into a greased jellyroll pan and bake for 25–30 minutes. Cool and reserve.

Mousse mixture

1 lb. semisweet chocolate, coarsely chopped (Callebaut)
4 oz. unsalted butter (Land-o-Lakes)
2 cups heavy cream, lightly whipped (Schepps)

Melt the chopped semisweet chocolate with the butter over medium-low heat. Fold in the lightly whipped cream; reserve.

$1^1/_2$ oz. Chambord
$1^1/_2$ oz. simple syrup (equal parts sugar and water)
1 pt. raspberries
2 oz. shaved white chocolate (Callebaut)
2 oz. shaved semisweet chocolate (Callebaut)
Almond Brittle (recipe follows)

To assemble:
Take four circular tin molds, 2 inches deep and 3 inches in diameter (they are kind of like deep biscuit cutters), and line with parchment paper. (Bruce Molzan found these molds in Paris, but says that you can also use PVC piping material.)

Place a layer of chocolate cake at bottom of each mold. Drizzle each layer of cake with Chambord and some of the simple syrup. Place raspberries on top of cake.

Divide the chocolate mousse evenly on top of each mold and pack down.

Chop up leftover chocolate cake into cubes and sprinkle on top of chocolate mixture. Sprinkle white and semisweet chocolate shavings over each dessert and refrigerate for 2 hours.

Unmold and top with chopped Almond Brittle. Serve at room temperature.

Optional: Raspberry, mango, and chocolate sauce garnish.

Almond brittle

1 cup granulated sugar
$^1/_2$ cup chopped almonds

Over medium heat, cook sugar until brown but not burned. Add almonds and continue cooking about 5 minutes more. Pour mixture into buttered sheet pan. Let cool and chop into small pieces.

Daniel O'Leary

Born December 12, 1954, in Charlestown, Massachusetts, Daniel O'Leary received his culinary training at the Culinary Institute of America. His favorite celebration is St. Patrick's Day; as a boy he wanted to be named Patrick. For birthdays, it's a German chocolate cake, and in the kitchen he wears clogs.

Chef O'Leary likes to cook everything. His favorite dish to eat is his mother's New England boiled dinner.

His worst culinary disaster occurred in Washington, D.C.:

"I was with Dean Fearing, preparing an outside seated diplomatic dinner for George Shultz and 300 guests. All the tables were completely set with china, crystal, and silver under a tent. About 30 minutes before the party began, a huge wind blew down half the tent, knocking down all of the tables and shattering about half the glassware. Somehow, everyone pitched in and got it set up again so George Shultz and the diplomats never knew.

"As to my most embarrassing culinary moment, it must have been so bad that I forgot it."

He remembered the best culinary moment as the Crescent Court First Annual Food and Wine Gala.

Chef O'Leary likes to whistle jazz, opera, popular, and western music.

When asked to define junk food, he said it was "any food that holds more grease than my car. I definitely eat it."

Aphorisms of Daniel O'Leary

1. Enjoy and take pride in your job.
2. In good cooking, there are no shortcuts.
3. In cooking, do simple, not overprepared foods with balanced flavors.

CHEF DANIEL O'LEARY

Beau Nash in the Crescent Court
400 Crescent Court
Dallas
(214) 871-3200

Menu

Artichoke-Corn Chowder

Long Sauvignon Blanc or Llano Estacado Signature White

Spicy Squid Salad with Mizuna Greens
and Wasabi Vinaigrette

Eberle Chardonnay or Etude Pinot Noir

Montasio Crusted Veal with Smoked Tomato Ratatoulli

Fisher Coach Insignia Cabernet Sauvignon or Opus One

Almond Wafers with White Chocolate Mousse
and Raspberry Sauce

Coffee

Llano Estacado Texas Champagne Brut

ARTICHOKE-CORN CHOWDER

Serves 6–8

3 strips smoked bacon cut in julienne
1½ medium onions, small dice
2 stalks celery, small dice
4 cups chicken stock
1 large white potato
Kernels from 2 medium ears of corn
3 large artichoke bottoms, small dice
2 cups heavy cream
3 dashes Tabasco sauce
2 dashes Worcestershire sauce
Salt and pepper to taste

Render bacon in a hot 2-qt. saucepan until brown. Add onions and celery; cook until onions become translucent without browning. Add chicken stock and bring to boil. Allow to simmer for 10 minutes. Add potato, corn, and artichokes; let simmer until potato is cooked approximately 10 minutes. Add cream and bring to a boil. Season with Tabasco, Worcestershire, salt and pepper, and serve.

SPICY SQUID SALAD WITH MIZUNA GREENS AND WASABI VINAIGRETTE

Serves 6–8

Step #1

1½ lbs. squid bodies, cut into rings
Marinate in:
1 cup olive oil
1 clove chopped garlic
1 large chopped shallot
½ tsp. chopped cilantro
½ tsp. chopped basil
¼ cup balsamic vinaigrette
Fresh bread crumbs

Let stand in marinade for 2–3 hours, then drain and toss in fresh bread crumbs until coated.

Step #2

In a blender or food processor, blend together until smooth:

1 tbsp. Wasabi horseradish powder diluted with 1 tbsp. water
1 small clove garlic, chopped
1 small shallot, chopped
½ tsp. lemon grass, chopped
¼ cup plain yogurt
2 tbsp. rice wine vinaigrette (unsalted)
Salt to taste

Step #3

Pick and clean mizuna greens; any other type of salad greens may be substituted.

Step #4

Fry squid in vegetable oil until golden brown and crispy. Drain on paper towels. Arrange greens on plates with squid around greens. Drizzle Wasabi vinaigrette over greens and squid and serve.

MONTASIO CRUSTED VEAL WITH SMOKED TOMATO RATATOULLI

Serves 6

1/2 cup fine grated montasio cheese (parmesan may be substituted)
1/4 cup fresh bread crumbs
Salt and pepper
12 veal loin medallions (2 1/2 oz. each)
1 oz. olive oil

Mix grated cheese and bread crumbs together.

Salt and pepper veal. Roll veal in bread crumb mixture until coated.

Heat olive oil in a sauté pan. Sauté veal until medium, approximately 3–4 minutes on each side.

Smoked tomato ratatoulli

3 large tomatoes, peeled, seeded, and diced
1 large onion
1 large zucchini
1 large yellow squash
3 cloves garlic
1 medium eggplant
1 red bell pepper, seeded
1 yellow bell pepper, seeded
1 green bell pepper, seeded
1 cup chicken stock
1/2 tsp. chopped oregano
1/2 tsp. chopped basil

Smoke diced tomatoes over mesquite or hickory for approximately 15 minutes. This may be done in a commercial smoker or on a covered barbecue grill.

Cut all vegetables into 1/2-inch dice. Heat olive oil in a heavy skillet. Sauté eggplant first until brown and remove and drain on paper towels. Add remaining vegetables and sauté until onions become translucent. Add tomatoes and chicken stock. Simmer 5 minutes; add herbs and let cook 5 more minutes.

Put ratatoulli on plate, place veal on top, and serve.

ALMOND WAFERS WITH WHITE CHOCOLATE MOUSSE AND RASPBERRY SAUCE

White chocolate mousse

7 oz. white chocolate
1½ cups heavy cream
½ cup egg whites
2 oz. sugar

Melt chocolate over a hot water bath. Remove from heat and cool down.

Whip heavy cream to soft peak; set aside. Mix sugar and whites to semi-stiff meringue.

Fold meringue vigorously into the cooled chocolate. Next fold in the whipped heavy cream. Mix well.

Almond wafer

8 oz. sugar
1 oz. all-purpose flour
4 large eggs
8 oz. sliced almonds (not roasted)

Mix sugar and flour. Add eggs and mix with fork. Fold in almond slices until completely mixed.

Grease cookie sheet well and spread 1 forkful of mix onto greased area into circle. Place in preheated oven at 375–400 degrees and bake until golden brown.

Use metal spatula to loosen from pan. While still hot, use cookie cutter for desired shape.

To assemble:
Coat wafer with mousse and raspberries; place another wafer on top and repeat procedure. Put third wafer on top and serve with Raspberry Sauce (recipe follows).

Raspberry sauce

(makes approximately 2 cups)

1 cup sugar
1 cup water
1 cup raspberries

Combine sugar and water together; bring to a boil, stirring constantly for approximately 3–4 minutes until sugar is dissolved.

In a food processor, purée 1 cup raspberries and strain through sieve. Stir into sugar/water mixture off of heat and let cool until ready for use.

Michel Bernard Platz

A native of Alsace, France (born on July 12, 1956), Michel Platz is not addicted to chocolate. He would prefer an Alsatian plum or mirabelle tart for his birthday.

Chef Platz started his three-year apprenticeship at age fourteen under Chef Jean Paul Koenig at the Hostellerie St. Barnabe in Alsace.

"It was a very strict and hard three years," he says, "but when I look back, I am very grateful because it has helped me a lot."

Christmas Eve is his favorite celebration because it brings back a lot of memories from his childhood.

"The tree was put up that morning by my mother, we had dinner, went to mass, and then opened the presents afterward. It was always a very exciting day and I still love it."

One pleasure for Chef Platz is relaxing in the office after everyone has gone at night.

"This is when I order or do paperwork or recipes. I also like taking care of the edible flowers without disturbances in the morning before anyone comes to work."

He likes cooking Alsatian foods and preparing the dishes served at L'Entrecote with edible flowers, his hallmark. His favorite dish to eat is one cooked by his mother: fresh baked tomato with ground meat, herbs, and fresh tomato sauce.

His best culinary moment was when he received a five-star award by the *Dallas Morning News* in 1987.

His most difficult preparation was the dinner in New York for the American Institute of Wine and Food in April 1988. It was a dinner and seminar on edible flowers.

"The hardest part was making sure that all flowers and herbs (flown from Texas to New York) made it there in good condition," he said. "The wonderful help and friendly atmosphere made it successful."

Chef Platz thinks the best shortcut is to spend a couple of days making basic stocks, reducing them well, and putting them in ice cube trays in the freezer for instant use when needed. His best substitute is mussel stock for fish stock, which he personally prefers in his fish sauces.

A fortune teller told him that his dream of someday owning his own restaurant would come true.

Aphorisms of Michel Platz

1. Learn and love the profession. There is so much to know to reach the top.
2. Know when the cooking flavors of ingredients have to be respected.
3. Be spontaneous. Spontaneity allows creativity and originality.
4. Respect the value, flavor, and other important factors of the particular dish being prepared. The whole composition must be respected.

CHEF MICHEL BERNARD PLATZ

L'Entrecote, Loews Anatole
2201 Stemmons Freeway
Dallas — (214) 748-1200

Menu

Terrine of Crabmeat in Gelee and Medallions in Salad and
Yellow Bell Pepper Coulis with Tarragon
Château St. Jean Sauvignon Blanc "La Petite Etoile"
or Messina Hof Chenin Blanc

Venison Consommé with Pearl Barley,
Curled Cabbage with Venison Mousse
and Pleurotte Mushrooms
Joseph Phelps Chardonnay or Gundlach-Bundschu Rhinefarm Merlot
Chilled Nasturtium Red Wine

Sautéed Loin and Roasted Leg of Rabbit
Stuffed with Liver and Pecans, Roasted Truffle Sauce
and Finished with Carrot Purée
Jordan Cabernet Sauvignon or Sterling Merlot

Green Asparagus and Baby Corn Salad
with Scrambled Quail Eggs and Pickled Red Roses
and Honey, Ginger, and Rose Vinaigrette
Hacienda Chenin Blanc or Clos du Val Semillon

Warm Raspberry Pie with Cinnamon Soufflé
and Fromage Blanc Ice Cream or
Rose Geranium Parfait with Rosemary Cream Anglaise
Coffee
Roederer Estate Brut

YELLOW BELL PEPPER COULIS WITH TARRAGON

Approximately 7 portions

4 sliced shallots
3 diced yellow bell peppers
2 oz. unsalted butter
Taste of fresh ground white pepper from the mill
Taste of salt
1 oz. tarragon vinegar
8 oz. dry white wine
16 oz. mussel stock (recipe follows)
8 oz. heavy cream
1 tbsp. fresh chopped tarragon

Slice the shallots and dice the yellow bell peppers. Place the butter in a warm pan and sauté (without giving any color) the shallots and the peppers slowly for a couple of minutes. Season with some pepper and a touch of salt. Deglaze the pan with the tarragon vinegar and the white wine, then add the mussel stock. Cook slowly for 10 minutes; add the cream and cook again.

Once the bell peppers are cooked, place them in the blender, and blend well. Check the seasoning and adjust if necessary. Pass mixture through a fine strainer, into a mixing bowl, and cool completely. It should be only slightly thick. If too thick add a little touch of mussel stock. When completely cold add the fresh chopped tarragon and let it sit for a few hours (or overnight to get the flavor out of the tarragon).

Take only the amount of coulis you need each time, and leave the rest in the refrigerator. It will keep very well for a few days.

Fresh mussel stock

10 oz. fresh fennel (or 1 oz. of 2 anise seeds)
10 oz. shallots
10 oz. white of leeks
4 oz. fresh butter
10 lbs. mussels
Fresh ground white pepper from the mill (to taste)
1/2 liter white vermouth
2 liters dry white wine

Dice the fennels and shallots and slice the leeks. In a warm pot, sauté slowly with butter (do not give it any color) for about 5 minutes.

Clean the mussels by taking the beard away and scraping the rocks or shellfish attached. Wash the mussels under cold running water for a few minutes.

Place the mussels over the vegetables. Mix. Add fresh ground white pepper, vermouth, and wine (if you do not have fresh fennel, add the anise seeds at this time). Place a cover on top and let it cook slowly until the mussels are totally open.

Strain the stock through a fine strainer, and let it cool off totally before clarification. You should have about 3 liters of stock.

Note: For this recipe you will use only the stock, but you can reserve the mussel meat and use it in another dish.

Clarification

3 liters mussel stock
4.5 oz. celery, chopped very fine
4.5 oz. fennel, chopped very fine
4.5 oz. onions, chopped very fine
7 oz. egg whites
2.5 oz. lemon juice
1 pinch saffron
Taste of salt
Taste of white pepper from the mill
2 oz. Pernod

Place the cold mussel stock in a cold pot. Add all other ingredients, and mix very well. (It is important to use a pot with a thick bottom so it does not have a chance to stick and burn while cooking.)

Place the pot on the stove and bring it slowly to a boil. Stir occasionally (slowly) to make sure it does not stick to the bottom, but when it starts simmering on the side do not stir anymore. Keep a close eye, as it should not boil too quickly. With a wooden spatula you can bring the cooked egg whites gently from the side toward the middle on to the top of the raft. It will give the stock a better chance to simmer totally clear. Taste and adjust the seasoning, if necessary. Let simmer or steep for 20 minutes.

Take the pot away from the heat slowly and strain the clarified stock carefully through a fine cheesecloth or large coffee filter. The stock should have a nice lemon color.

CRAB TERRINE

Mussel gelee

2.5 gelatin leaves
10 oz. clarified mussel stock (hot)
6 oz. king crab leg meat, diced
Taste of fresh ground white pepper
Taste of salt (if necessary)
4 moulds (2 oz. each)

Place the gelatin leaves in a bowl with cold water (about 8 oz.) and let it soak for about 10 minutes. Take all but 1 oz. of water away, and place the bowl with the gelatin over hot water to melt it totally. Once done, place in it the 10 oz. of hot mussel stock. Mix it nicely. Transfer it into a clean bowl, and place it in the refrigerator. In the meantime, clean the crabmeat of any shells it may have.

When the stock is almost set like gelee, mix the crabmeat in, add a couple of twists of fresh white pepper, and check if it needs any salt.

Place it in the moulds and let it set for about 30 minutes in the refrigerator. Take out of the mould as needed, but it cannot be kept for more than 3 days.

CRAB SALAD

1 oz. per person crab leg meat
1/4 oz. per person tarragon vinaigrette (recipe follows)
Pinch chopped parsley
Taste of fresh ground white pepper

Slice the crab legs into medallions, add the parsley, fresh ground white pepper, and tarragon vinaigrette. Mix well.

Tarragon vinaigrette

16 oz. Mazola oil
16 oz. olive oil
2 oz. fine chopped shallots
2 oz. fine chopped tarragon
1 tbsp. Dijon mustard
5 1/4 oz. tarragon (or champagne) vinegar
4 oz. fresh lemon juice
Taste of salt
Taste of fresh ground white pepper

Mix all ingredients together very well, and let it set at least one day minimum so the ingredients have a chance to give their full flavor.

Final presentation (serves 4):

4 oz. yellow bell pepper and tarragon coulis
4 crab terrines
4 oz. crab salad
4 tarragon branches, 2 inches long
4 blue pansies
4 x 3 tips small green asparagus tips, 1 1/2 inches long

For each serving, place yellow bell pepper coulis on the bottom of the plate in a nice circle. In the center of the coulis, toward the left, place the crab terrine, and toward the right place the crab salad (make sure the salad is not running over with vinaigrette). On the top, between the terrine and salad, place 3 asparagus tips, and on the bottom part, place a branch of fresh tarragon and a nice blue pansy.

VENISON CONSOMMÉ WITH PEARL BARLEY, CURLED CABBAGE WITH VENISON MOUSSE AND PLEUROTTE MUSHROOMS

8 Servings

Venison stock

12 lbs. venison bones
1 lb. carrots, chopped
1 lb. celery branch, chopped
1 lb. onions, chopped
1 lb. tomato, fresh, chopped
1 lb. white mushrooms
2 cups vegetable oil
5 oz. parsley stems
1 oz. fresh thyme
1/2 oz. bay leaves
3 pieces garlic cloves
1 tbsp. cracked black peppercorn
4 gallons cold water

Roast the venison bones in the oven. Sauté all vegetables in oil and give it a nice light brown color. Place the bones in a pot, add the spices, the vegetables, and cover with the cold water. Let it cook for about 4 to 5 hours slowly. Clean often the top of the stock.

When ready, strain the stock and cover the bones with water a second time. Cook again for 4 hours.

Strain the second boil. (Venison bones, as veal, always have enough flavor to make two boils.)

Place both boils together and reduce by half. Let it cool off. You should have about 3 gallons left.

Venison consommé clarification

3 gallons venison stock (should give you at the end 2–2 1/2 gallons of consommé)
2 lbs. ground venison meat
20 oz. fine chopped carrot
20 oz. celery
20 oz. leeks
20 oz. tomato
20 oz. egg whites
1/2 oz. fresh thyme
10 bay leaves
Juice of 2 fresh lemons
Fresh ground pepper from the mill, a few twists

Place all ingredients except stock (use a pot with thick bottom) in a pot. Add then the cold venison stock (clean any fat away, until you find the clear stock). Mix everything very well. Place on the stove and slowly bring to a boil.

Stir once in a while slowly to make sure nothing is sticking on the bottom. When you see simmering on the side, do not mix anymore, but keep a close eye to make sure it does not boil too quickly. With a wooden spatula, you can bring gently the cooked egg whites from the side toward the center on top of the others.

Once the consommé is totally clear, get a small taste of it to check the seasoning, and make all corrections.

Strain the consommé through a very fine cheesecloth.

Note: With all the work of making a consommé, it is better to make a larger quantity and use it later. You can keep it in the refrigerator or even freeze it in smaller quantity. Keep no longer than two months in the freezer.

Venison mousse

1 lb. venison meat
2 oz. Madeira
2 oz red Port
4 oz. cup chopped parsley
1 tsp. chopped thyme leaves
Taste of salt
Taste of fresh ground white pepper from the mill
4 whole eggs

Clean the fat and sliver skin off the meat. Grind the meat twice to get it very fine. Place the meat in a mixing bowl and add all ingredients. Mix it very well. Sauté a small amount and taste. Correct the seasoning if necessary.

Preparation:

1 leaf curled green cabbage
3 pieces wild mushroom (pleurottes)
1 tsp. pearl barley
1 bowl corn blossoms

Blanch the curled cabbage leaves in salted water and place them on a towel to dry them out. Place each leaf on the table, and pipe the mousse in the center with a tube #4.

Roll the cabbage until there are 2 layers around the mousse. Steam slowly for 10 minutes over simmering, seasoned water (salt, a branch of thyme, and 2 oz. of white wine).

Julienne the pleurotte mushrooms (cut in slivers). Cook the pearl barley in lightly salted boiling water.

Final presentation:
For each serving, cut 5 slices of mousse and arrange in half circle in a deep soup plate. Garnish with the julienne of raw mushrooms, sprinkle 1 tsp. of pearl barley around.

Place the corn blossom in the center (if none available, use a nice branch of flowering thyme).

Present the plate, and gently pour in the hot consommé (about 8 oz. serving per person).

Note: If you have some raw venison mousse left, you can pipe it in film paper, roll it the size needed, and place it in the freezer. Then when needed, just defrost and roll in blanched cabbage. Steam as needed.

CHILLED NASTURTIUM RED WINE

Step One:

Marinate 1/2 liter of Syrah wine with 2 dozen nasturtiums for about 2 weeks in the refrigerator. Check the flavor; by then you should have a good nasturtium-flavored wine.

Step Two:

1 liter Syrah red wine
8 oz. syrup (1 liter water with 2 lbs. sugar boiled together)
8 oz. water
Juice of 1 1/2 fresh oranges
Peelings of one orange
1 cinnamon stick
10 cloves
4 bay leaves
1/4 tsp. cracked black peppercorn

Boil slowly all ingredients for 15 minutes. Let it rest overnight with all ingredients. Strain before serving.

Step Three:

When ready to use, mix about 1 liter of the spiced wine and 1/2 liter of the nasturtium wine together in a bowl. Place the bowl over ice and serve very chilled. Present it with 1 or 2 fresh nasturtiums to soak inside the wine for a few minutes. Eat the nasturtiums and enjoy the chilled wine.

Note: Chill the glasses in the freezer before serving the wine (serve about 3 oz. per person).

SAUTÉED LOIN AND ROASTED LEG OF RABBIT STUFFED WITH LIVER AND PECANS, ROASTED TRUFFLE SAUCE AND FINISHED WITH CARROT PURÉE

Serves 4

Deboning the rabbit

2 whole rabbits weighing 3 lbs. each

Remove the front and back legs by cutting at the shoulder and hip joints. Reserve the legs for later. Remove the loins from the carcass by cutting along each side of the back bones and down the rib bones. Remove fat and sliver skins from the loins.

Debone the thigh by cutting along the bone to the joint. Do not remove the bone from the calf.

Chop the carcass and shoulder bones, and roast until brown in the oven. Save these for sauce.

Liver and pecan stuffing for rabbit leg

4 oz. rabbit liver
1 oz. bacon cut in fine julienne
1/2 tsp. finely chopped shallots
1/2 tsp. brandy
1/2 tsp. Port red
1/2 tsp. Madeira
1/2 tsp. fresh thyme leaves
1 oz. pecans
1 egg white

Dice the fresh rabbit liver and place it in a bowl. Add the julienne of bacon, shallots, wines, and fresh thyme leaves. Mix well, and let marinate overnight.

Chop the pecans. Sauté them quickly in touch of butter for a few seconds. Let cool.

Strain out all the marinade from the liver and discard. Mix the egg white and the pecans with the liver; add salt and a few twists of fresh ground white pepper from the mill. Sauté a small amount and taste. Correct the seasoning if necessary.

Final preparation:

4 pieces lace fat (triangle shape, 6-inch side)
4 oz. liver stuffing
4 pieces rabbit legs, deboned

Place the lace fat on the table, with the rabbit leg on top. Open the thigh and place about 1 oz. of liver stuffing in the center; cover with the side meat. Roll the lace fat over to hold the leg together and let it rest in the refrigerator.

Roasted truffle sauce finished with a carrot purée

For purée: Dice 8 oz. of carrot and cook well in seasoned water. Then strain and blend thoroughly. Chill.

For sauce:

4 oz. diced tomato
6 oz. diced carrots
6 oz. diced shallots
6 oz. diced celery
Thyme branch, about 2
6 oz. truffle juice
6 oz. Madeira wine
4 oz. vegetable oil
8 oz. Pinot Noir
2 qts. water

Marinate the vegetables and thyme in the truffle juice and madeira overnight.

In a hot pot add the oil and roast the marinated vegetables until golden brown in the oven. Then add the roasted rabbit bones. Deglaze with half of the marinade, the Pinot Noir, and the cold water. Cook slowly for 1 hour, until it is reduced by one-third.

Final presentation:

4 stuffed rabbit legs
Second half marinade
20 oz. of rabbit stock
3 tbsp. carrot purée
2 tsp. chopped truffle
4 rabbit loins
4 tbsp. fresh butter
Taste of salt
Taste of fresh ground white peppercorn

In a hot pan, sauté the seasoned rabbit legs in 2 tbsp. butter until golden brown then finish in the oven, for 10 minutes at 400 degrees. When ready, remove meat and set aside. Then remove the fat and deglaze with the rest of the marinade. Reduce, then add the rabbit stock. Let it simmer down to two-thirds, and add carrot purée to finish. Check the seasoning. Then add the chopped truffle.

Sauté the seasoned rabbit loin in 2 tbsp. butter (keep it pink). When ready to serve, slice the legs and place on the right side of the plate, and the sliced rabbit loin on the left side. Pour the sauce around the leg and the loin.

Sprinkle some chopped parsley on top, and garnish with a branch of thyme and edible daisies.

GREEN ASPARAGUS AND BABY CORN SALAD WITH SCRAMBLED QUAIL EGGS AND PICKLED RED ROSES

Pickled red roses

The red roses are to be used from either a special farm of edible flowers or from your garden. However, there cannot be any insecticide used during the growing of the flower.

Vinegar for pickling

Bring to a boil 8 oz. of champagne vinegar, 4 oz. of water, and 1 oz. of sugar.

Rinse the roses (preferably red, to give a nice color to the vinegar) and place in a bowl. Pour over the hot vinegar, let it cool off. Marinate for a minimum of 2 weeks. As time goes by, you may add fresh rose to the marinade as often as you want. Keep up to a month and a half with the same roses, then strain the vinegar. Dispose of the old roses. Check the flavor and color of the vinegar. It should have a pretty red color and the flavor of the rose. If flavor is not strong enough, keep adding roses until you like the vinegar.

Note: When vinegar is ready, pickle for a couple of hours the whole rose or petals to be used as garnish.

Any color roses are nice for the vinegar base. However, red ones add a nice touch of color. For garnish, the red roses are the *only* ones that will stay firm, fresh looking, and flavorful once pickled.

Honey, ginger and rose vinaigrette

3 cups Mazola oil
1 cup rose vinegar
2 tbsp. shallots, finely chopped
1 tbsp. Dijon mustard
1 tsp. ginger, finely chopped
1 or 2 tsp. honey (to taste)
1 tsp. soya sauce
Taste of salt and white pepper from the mill
Tabasco, a few drops

Mix all ingredients together and let rest for a couple days for flavor. Strain the vinaigrette in fine strainer and check the seasoning.

Note: It is easier to make a vinaigrette in larger quantities than actually needed, and keep it for later use.

Presentation (serves 1):

7 pieces green asparagus (4½ inches long)
3 pieces baby corn *(fresh)*
1½ oz. Honey, Ginger, and Rose Vinaigrette
6–7 Pickled Red Rose Petals
3 pieces quail eggs
1 piece branch of thyme

Peel and cook 7 green asparagus and 3 baby corn *al dente*. Cut the baby corn in half (lengthwise) and place in a deep plate with the asparagus. Season with a touch of salt and fresh ground white pepper. Cover with some vinaigrette and let marinate for 10 minutes.

Place the asparagus on the left side of the plate (tips down) and the baby corn (tips down) on the right. Garnish the baby corn with some blanched corn husks underneath.

Cover the salad with an extra touch of vinaigrette. Garnish with a few pickled rose petals.

Crack three quail eggs per person. Add a touch of cream, salt, and white pepper. Beat well. Cook them softly scrambled. Place eggs at the top of the salad. Then add a nice small branch of fresh thyme, and one quail egg shell.

Serve the salad at room temperature with hot scrambled eggs.

Note: When cracking the eggs, you will need to save one shell per salad as garnish. Cut the point with a knife and shake the egg out.

WARM RASPBERRY PIE WITH CINNAMON SOUFFLÉ AND FROMAGE BLANC ICE CREAM

Fromage blanc ice cream

1 lb. fresh fromage blanc (fresh soft creamed cheese)
1½ qt. cream anglaise (recipe follows)
4 oz. sugar
1 oz. kirsch

Mix all ingredients and place mixture in ice cream machine. It is important to take it out as soon as it starts to get fairly firm, to prevent a grainy texture. Place in the freezer to harden.

Cream anglaise

½ qt. milk
½ qt. heavy cream
2 vanilla beans (cut in half)
8 oz. sugar
12 egg yolks

Combine the milk, cream, and vanilla beans. Bring this mixture to a boil. In a separate bowl, mix the sugar and egg yolks and beat over hot water until fluffy. Slowly add the hot cream mixture. Place in a pot and allow mixture to thicken slightly over low heat. Strain through a fine strainer, returning the vanilla beans to the mixture. Let rest overnight.

Sweet pie dough

5½ oz. sugar
10 oz. fresh butter
1 lb. cake flour
1 whole egg
Taste of vanilla extract
Touch of lemon extract

Mix all ingredients together. Let mixture rest at least 30 minutes.

Take about 1/3 of the dough and roll to a thickness of 1/8 inch. Cut 4 circles of 5-inch diameter. Place them on a buttered baking tray and pre-cook for 3 minutes at 350 degrees. Let cool.

Wrap the rest of the dough in plastic wrap and place in the refrigerator for later use.

Soufflé base

2 oz. pastry flour
1 whole egg and 5 egg yolks (combined to mix with flour)
10 oz. milk
3 oz. sugar
1 oz. butter
Touch of vanilla extract
2 egg yolks (added at the end)

In a bowl, mix the flour and the eggs. Bring the milk, sugar, butter, and vanilla extract to a boil. Pour this over the flour and egg mixture. Mix well. Place back in the pot and cook for 10 minutes, stirring constantly.

Remove from heat and add the last 2 yolks. Mix thoroughly. Let cool.

Final preparation (for 2 servings):

2 tbsp. soufflé base
1 tsp. ground cinnamon
1/2 tsp. fine sugar
2 egg whites
4 pre-cooked sweet dough circles
2 pts. fresh raspberries

Place the soufflé base, cinnamon, and some of the sugar in a mixing bowl; mix thoroughly. Whip the egg whites and gently add them to the soufflé base.

Place the pie circle on a lightly buttered baking tray. Evenly spread 1 1/2 tbsp. of soufflé base on each one. Arrange raspberries on top.

Sprinkle a cinnamon sugar mixture over the raspberries and bake in oven at 350 degrees for about 10 minutes.

Presentation of Marzipan Bee:
Mix about 2 oz. of marzipan paste with a touch of yellow food coloring. Make the oval body about 1 1/2 inches long. With the back of a knife make an indention around the body to form shape of a head. With a very fine paintbrush and black food coloring make the stripes on the body and two eyes. With the thumb, press some marzipan to make two teardrop-shaped wings. Form the bee.

When the raspberry pies are ready, place them on a warm plate and garnish with one marzipan bee. Add one scoop of fromage blanc ice cream on each pie and serve immediately.

Note: Instead of fromage blanc ice cream, you can use vanilla ice cream.

ROSE GERANIUM PARFAIT WITH ROSEMARY CREAM ANGLAISE

Serves 10

1 dozen rose geranium leaves
2 dozen rose geranium blossoms
1/2 qt. heavy cream (35%)
7 egg yolks
6 oz. water (will be reduced by half)
4 oz. sugar
Juice of 1 fresh orange
1 oz. kirsch
10 moulds (4 oz. each)
10 rose geranium blossoms (garnish)

Note: Make sure that neither the blossoms nor the rose geranium leaves were sprayed by insecticide. You can find them at special farms that grow edible flowers.

Marinate 1/2 of the rose geranium leaves and the rose geranium for a couple days in the cream.

Place the egg yolks in a mixing bowl and whip until they are white and have a thick texture.

In the meantime, boil 6 oz. of water, with the rest of rose geranium leaves and half of the sugar. Reduce by half; remove leaves and add remaining sugar. Cook until the texture is like thick syrup (test by taking a small portion and placing it in cold water; it is ready if a soft ball forms). Then pour it slowly into the whipped yolks and let it whip until the whole mixture gets cold. Add the fresh orange juice. Strain the mousse through a strainer to remove any pieces of sugar lumps.

To extract color and flavor from the flowers, blend the cream mixture quickly. (Do not allow this to become warm.) Strain through a fine strainer and whip until firm.

Softly mix the cream mixture, the egg mousse, and the kirsch with a spatula. You should have a nice soft pink color. If necessary, you may squeeze a few drops of raspberry juice, to give more color.

Place the whole geranium blossom on the bottom of the mould, upside down, and pour the parfait mixture over slowly. Place in the freezer overnight.

Note: The flower on the parfait will stay nice for a couple of days in the freezer. If you wish to make enough to keep longer, I suggest you place the petals in the middle of the parfait while filling it, and then garnish with a fresh blossom on the top when serving it later on.

Light rosemary cream anglaise

1/2 qt. milk
1/2 qt. heavy cream
2 vanilla beans (cut in half)
1/2 oz. rosemary leaves
8 oz. sugar
12 egg yolks

Bring the milk and cream to a boil with the vanilla beans and the rosemary. Mix the sugar and the yolks in a mixing bowl, and beat over hot water until fluffy. Then slowly add the hot milk and cream. Mix again well in a pot over low heat until slightly thicker. Strain through a fine strainer and place the vanilla beans and rosemary back into the mixture. Let it rest overnight, then strain again.

Note: If you are not a fan of rosemary, you can leave it out and just make a plain cream anglaise.

White chocolate harp

Melt 4 oz. of white chocolate in a bowl over warm water.

Place wax paper on a flat tray over the harp design. With a piping bag and a #2 tube, pipe the 6 center lines first. Then with a #4 tube, pipe the outside lines of the harp. (Give it the same thickness, so it will hold nicely.) With the same tube, fill the square for the base completely.

Let it all set in a cold place, but not in the refrigerator.

When ready to use, place some slightly melted white chocolate on the base, and place the harp on top. Place an edible Dianthus blossom and a tip of mint on the soft chocolate. Hold the harp by the thick part until totally set. Once completed, it has to be handled with care.

Dark chocolate violin

Melt 2 oz. sweet dark chocolate and 1 oz. white chocolate in separate bowls over warm water.

Place wax paper on a flat tray over the violin design. With a piping bag and #3 tube, pipe the dark chocolate inside the violin shape design. Let it set in a cold place but not in the refrigerator. When cold, pipe the top design in white chocolate with a #2 tube.

Once the work is finished, handle with care.

Presentation (serves 1):

Icing sugar
2 oz. rosemary cream anglaise
1 rose geranium parfait
1 white chocolate harp
1 dark chocolate violin
1 rosemary tip (1-inch long)
1 rose geranium leaf
6–7 small edible flowers

Using a fine strainer, sprinkle a thin coat of powdered sugar on the border of the plate, until covered. Place the rosemary cream anglaise in a circle on the bottom of the plate. Demould the parfait and place it in the center.

Garnish by placing the white harp toward the top left of the plate (the flower looking toward the front) and the dark violin at the front, tilted a little toward the right and partially lying against the parfait. Finish by placing the green herbs and the edible blossoms and place nicely all around the parfait.

For me, this dish is very special. I think it tastes just like the actual taste of the geranium and it looks wonderful.

Elmar Prambs

Elmar Prambs was born in West Germany on August 11, 1957. He served a three-year apprenticeship in Garmisch-Partenkirchen, Germany.

Like several of the chefs, he avoids fortune tellers, wears clogs in the kitchen, loves Black Forest cake (with lots of Kirsch in it) for his birthday, enjoys New Year's Eve (but really hates New Year's Day), likes barbecuing with friends and family and spending more than sixty hours in the kitchen.

His most esteemed honor is being part of the Four Seasons team. He also mentioned being a medal winner at the Culinary Olympics in Frankfurt in 1984.

The chef's German heritage doubtlessly influenced his tastes. His favorite dish to cook is Rosemary Braised Duckling (simmered in its own juices) and his favorite thing to eat is Beef Roulade with Braised Red Cabbage.

He answered the question about his worst disaster: "I'll never tell — and hope no one ever noticed."

The best culinary moment, he recalls, was "back at our Grand Opening Party for the Four Seasons in 1987, when it was all set up and done. And my most difficult preparation was getting ready for the 1989 Texas Hill Country Wine and Food Festival."

A tip he offers to cooks is: "Only cook what you like to eat yourself. It is safer that way." And the best shortcut is "the one nobody finds out that you've used."

About junk food, he defines it as candy, sweets, cookies, popcorn, and chips. And does he eat it?

"Of course, I love it."

Aphorisms of Elmar Prambs

1. There's no substitute if you are able to get the real thing. If you can't get the real thing, prepare something else.
2. Don't take life too seriously; it's too short. Enjoy good food and wine and a cheerful spirit.

CHEF ELMAR PRAMBS

Riverside Cafe at Four Seasons Austin
98 San Jacinto Boulevard
Austin
(512) 478-4500

Menu

Lobster Ravioli with Tomato Butter Sauce and Chives

Hacienda Clair de Lune Chardonnay or
Preston Dry Creek Chenin Blanc

Oysters in Pecan Crust

Mondavi Fumé Blanc or Bouchaine or Caymus Pinot Noir

Salmon Terrine

Sonoma-Cutrer Chardonnay Les Pierres or Iron Horse Pinot Noir

Veal Medallions, Basic Cream Sauce,
and Grilled Asiago Polenta

Fall Creek Cabernet Sauvignon or Joseph Phelps Cabernet Sauvignon

Roasted Pork Tenderloin, Port Wine Sauce,
and Corn Custard

Llano Estacado Cabernet Sauvignon or Jaeger Pinot Noir

Mocha Soufflé

Coffee

Van der Kamp Brut

LOBSTER RAVIOLI WITH TOMATO BUTTER SAUCE AND CHIVES

Serves 4

Ravioli dough

2½ cups flour
1 egg
2 tbsp. puréed cilantro
Water, enough to bind mixture

Combine flour, egg, and cilantro by hand or with a food processor. Add enough water for mixture to come together into a ball. Work pasta dough on floured surface until elastic and smooth; set aside.

Filling

4 (4-oz.) lobster tails (remove shell and devein)
¾ cup heavy cream
2 egg whites
1 tsp. brandy
1 tbsp. soft butter
Salt, pepper, cayenne
2 tbsp. diced chives

Cook 2 lobster tails in flavored stock until done (still moist). Let cool and dice in fine cubes. Place remaining 2 lobster tails into food processor and chop finely. Add other ingredients except chives. Blend well. Remove from food processor; place in bowl and mix in diced lobster meat and chives.

Roll out ravioli dough and cut into rounds. Between 2 rounds place a teaspoon of the filling. Secure and seal pasta rounds with an egg wash.

Drop ravioli in boiling chicken broth and simmer 7–10 minutes. Place on plate, cover with sauce, and garnish with sautéed tomatoes and chive spears.

Tomato butter sauce with chives

(Yield: 4–6 cups)

1½ cups dry white wine
2 tbsp. fresh lime juice
3 tbsp. diced shallots
1 tsp. tomato paste
½ lb. chilled, unsalted butter (cut into 20 pieces)
Salt and freshly ground white pepper
2 tbsp. diced chives

Combine wine, lime juice, shallots, and tomato paste in saucepan and cook over moderate heat until the liquid is reduced to about 2 tbsp. Remove the pan from the heat to cool slightly, then return to low heat and whisk in a few pieces of butter into reduction until the mixture looks creamy. Beat in the remaining butter, piece by piece. The finished sauce will be barely warm and have the soft fluid consistency of barely whipped cream. Season it to taste with salt and white pepper. Add diced chives and serve.

OYSTERS IN PECAN CRUST

1 Serving

5–6 oysters removed from shell
$^{1}/_{2}$ cup seasoned flour
1 egg beaten
$^{3}/_{4}$ cup ground pecans
1–2 oz. clarified butter

Drain the oysters from their liquid and pat dry. Roll the oysters (1) first in the seasoned flour; (2) next drop them into the beaten egg to moisten; (3) remove the oyster from the beaten egg and roll in the ground pecans. Sauté the pecan-crusted oysters in clarified butter over medium heat, browning 1 minute on both sides. Serve with Basil Butter Sauce.

Basil butter sauce

1 shallot minced
$^{1}/_{2}$ cup white wine (dry)
2 tbsp. heavy cream
6 tbsp. unsalted butter, cut into 6 pieces
1 tbsp. julienned fresh basil

Place the shallot and white wine in a small saucepan. Reduce by $^{3}/_{4}$. Add the heavy cream and reduce by $^{1}/_{2}$. Lower heat and whisk in the unsalted butter 1 piece at a time, making sure the sauce does not boil or get too cold. Season the sauce to taste with salt and pepper and add the julienned basil.

SALMON TERRINE

1 pkg. unflavored gelatin
$^{3}/_{4}$ cup heavy cream
$^{3}/_{4}$ lb. smoked salmon
6 tbsp. soft, unsalted butter
$^{1}/_{2}$ lime juice or lemon
2 tbsp. capers, drained
1 tbsp. red onion, small dice
2 tbsp. cooked egg white
2 tbsp. chopped parsley

Soften the gelatin in the cold heavy cream. Then place the gelatin/cream mixture over a double boiler to heat. While the cream is heating, place the smoked salmon in the food processor and blend until smooth. Add the soft butter to the salmon and process just enough to mix together well. Once the cream is warm, stir to dissolve all the gelatin and remove from the heat and let cool slightly. Add the gelatin/cream mixture to the smoked salmon with the food processor running. Process only enough to blend well. Remove salmon mixture from the food processor. Place into a bowl. Fold in the lime juice and remaining garnishes. Line a terrine with plastic wrap. Place salmon mixture in the terrine. Cover and refrigerate until firm, 6–8 hours. Unmold and slice.

VEAL MEDALLIONS, BASIC CREAM SAUCE, AND GRILLED ASIAGO POLENTA

Serves 4

12 (1 1/2-oz.) veal tenderloin medallions
Basil leaves and cilantro sprigs for garnish

Sauté veal medallions in butter until pink (about 2 minutes on each side). Season with salt and pepper.

Asiago polenta

4 shallots, minced
1 garlic clove, minced
3 cups chicken stock
2 cups heavy cream (32%)
2 oz. minced cilantro
1 1/2 cups cornmeal
1/2 cup grated asiago cheese

Sauté shallots and garlic in butter until golden brown. Add chicken stock, cream, and minced cilantro; bring to a boil. Then add cornmeal and asiago cheese, stirring frequently, and cook for about 3 minutes. Pour into a greased pan about 1-inch high and let cool. Cut out diamond-shaped pieces and cook on griddle until golden brown and hot.

Basil cream sauce

1 tbsp. shallots, chopped
1 tsp. garlic, chopped
1/2 cup mushrooms
1 cup dry white wine
2 cups cream (32%)
2 tbsp. basil leaves, fresh
Salt and pepper

Sauté shallots and garlic in butter; add mushrooms and remaining ingredients. Cook for about 10–15 minutes. Purée in blender until smooth. Adjust seasoning.

Vegetables

Use turned red beets, carrot balls, asparagus spears, cauliflower florets, strips of red bell peppers, broccoli.

Blanch all vegetables in salted boiling water separately. Chill in ice water. Reheat in chicken stock and sauté lightly in butter; add white pepper to taste.

Presentation:

Arrange the vegetables throughout a plate. Place sautéed veal medallions and asiago polenta in between the vegetables. Spoon Basil Cream Sauce over the veal. Garnish plate with basil and cilantro sprigs.

ROASTED PORK TENDERLOIN, PORT WINE SAUCE, AND CORN CUSTARD

Serves 4

4 (6-oz.) pork tenderloins

Salt and pepper

Season pork with salt and pepper and cook in a hot pan with 1 tbsp. olive oil until done, about 6–8 minutes.

Sauce

1½ cups veal stock*

½ cup Port wine

Cook for about 10 minutes; adjust seasoning (salt, pepper, and touch of cayenne pepper)

Corn custard

½ cup corn kernels
1 garlic clove, minced
4 whole eggs
1 cup cream (32%)
Salt and ground white pepper

Sauté corn and garlic in butter for about 4–5 minutes. Let cool. Whisk together eggs and cream; add corn and salt and pepper. Spoon mixture into lightly buttered 4-oz. molds. Bake in a water bath at 375 degrees for 15–18 minutes.

* If veal stock is not available, use packet gravy mix (Knorr brand is usually the best) and follow the instructions on the packet, then add 1 cup of red wine and 2 tbsp. of brandy, 2 bay leaves, and 1 tsp. crushed black peppercorn. Cook for another 10 minutes; strain through sieve.

Vegetables
Sauté pearl onions (fresh peeled), pecan halves, mushrooms cut in quarters, diced red, green and yellow bell peppers, diced tomatoes, and green peppercorns in butter. Season with salt and fresh ground pepper and add 2 tbsp. Port Wine Sauce and mix well.

Presentation:
On the plate, using radicchio leaf formed into a cup, spoon in the vegetables, spilling over onto the plate. Remove corn custard from mold and place brown side up on the plate. Ladle on sauce and arrange sliced pork loin (about 8–10 slices) over the sauce. Garnish with fresh rosemary sprig.

MOCHA SOUFFLÉ

Makes 8 soufflés

1 oz. soft butter
1 oz. sugar
1 oz. bread flour
5 oz. milk
3 egg yolks
3 tbsp. instant coffee
3 egg whites
2 oz. sugar

Boil the milk, pour in butter/sugar/flour mixture. Stir and bring back to a boil. Remove from heat and add 3 egg yolks and 3 tbsp. instant coffee. Let cool.

Whip the egg white with the sugar until soft peaks form. Fold into the cool mixture. Butter the inside of 8 individual soufflé molds and sprinkle with sugar, then pour in the mixture.

Bake in preheated oven at 425 degrees for about 12–15 minutes. Sprinkle top with powdered sugar and serve right away.

Stephan Pyles

A native of Big Spring, Texas (born March 6, 1952), Stephan Pyles has received numerous awards, recognitions, and honors for his superlative and unique cuisine. He is in demand constantly to demonstrate cooking methods as well as to prepare foods for events and gatherings of various sizes. A personable and dedicated self-taught chef, he has extraordinary talents.

Chef Pyles was awarded "Who's Who in Texas Food and Wine," was a *Cook's* magazine selection for its Who's Who roster, a *Nations Restaurant News* selection, and is in the City of Hope Hall of Fame and Fine Dining Hall of Fame. He was the first Texan to be named to *Cook's* Who's Who list (1985).

Like some other chefs, he wears sneakers in the kitchen. Among his favorite things are cooking pasta, celebrating July 4, eating honey-fried chicken, participating in "Meals on Wheels," gardening, swimming, and reading.

His best culinary moment was cooking with Luciano Pavarotti.

The chef's best tip to cooks is to taste, taste, taste! His suggested best shortcut is fast puff pastry.

He attributes his preference for Tex/Mex, Southern cooking, and barbecue to his Texas heritage and growing up in the Lone Star State:

"For me, cooking has always been a way of life. Because I was born into a restaurant family, I learned from an early age that nurturing someone was a very gratifying experience.

"Today my style of cooking is quite different from the food of my childhood, but the basic pleasure of nourishing has not changed. To walk into my dining room at Routh Street Cafe and see the many satisfied, smiling faces is a wonderful feeling.

"Today, cooking is also a creative outlet for me, much as music was in college. To plan a menu with a new combination of ingredients, then execute the dishes and see the contrasts of colors and taste the layers of textures and flavors is a feeling like no other in the world.

"It also gives me great pleasure to know that my talents can be used to help others that are less fortunate. In this country now we see celebrity chefs cooking to raise money for everything from cancer research to hunger relief to political causes. I think it is a moral obligation that we have to give back at least something in return for our success.

"It is a most wonderful life when what you do for a living seems so little like work."

CHEF STEPHAN PYLES

Routh Street Cafe
3005 Routh Street at Cedar Springs
Dallas
(214) 871-7161

Menu

Tamale Tart with Roasted Garlic Custard
and Gulf Coast Crab Meat

Ferrari-Carano Fumé Blanc or
Flora Springs Barrel Fermented Chardonnay

Filet of Salmon with Cilantro, Anchos, and Orange

Beaulieu Pinot Noir Los Carneros Reserve
or Robert Mondavi Chardonnay

Chipotle Lamb Chops with Creamed Corn Pudding
and Three Tomato Salsas

Freemark Abbey Bosche Cabernet
or Domaine Michel Cabernet Sauvignon

Warm Apple-Raisin Spice Cake with Caramel Sauce
and Vanilla Ice Cream

Renaissance Late Harvest White Riesling
Coffee
Hanns Kornell Brut

TAMALE TART WITH ROASTED GARLIC CUSTARD AND GULF COAST CRAB MEAT

Serves 10 as appetizer or 6 as main course

Roasted Garlic Custard (recipe follows)
1¼ cups masa harina
¾ cup yellow cornmeal
2 tsp. salt
¼ tsp. cayenne
2 tsp. cumin
10 tbsp. shortening
2 tbsp. red bell pepper purée
2 tbsp. ancho chile purée
2 tbsp. olive oil
4 tbsp. diced onion
10 oz. Gulf Coast Lump Crab Meat, carefully picked over
4 tbsp. diced red tomatoes
4 tbsp. diced yellow tomatoes
2 tbsp. cilantro
2 tsp. diced serrano chiles
Juice of 1 lime
Salt to taste

Recommended equipment: Electric hand mixer
Mixing bowl
9″ false-bottom tart pan
Bamboo steamer
Medium sauté pan

Make Roasted Garlic Custard mix and set aside (at room temperature) while preparing tart.

Combine dry ingredients (masa harina, cornmeal, salt, cayenne and cumin) and set aside. In a mixing bowl whip the shortening with hand mixer until light and fluffy. Gradually add dry ingredients and continue to whip until well blended and smooth. Whip in red pepper and ancho purées and form into a ball.

Pat the dough into a 9″ false-bottom tart pan and press to flatten on bottom and up sides. Fill with the roasted garlic custard mix and cover tart pan completely with plastic wrap. Place in bamboo steamer set over boiling water and steam for 25–30 minutes.

When tart is almost finished, heat the olive oil in a medium sauté pan until lightly smoking. Add the onions and sauté for 1 minute. Add crab meat, tomatoes, cilantro, serranos, and lime juice. Cook until warmed through (about 2 minutes). Place on top of tart and slice into pieces.

Roasted garlic custard

Makes 6 custards or fills tamale tart pan

1 tbsp. olive oil
6 large garlic cloves, peeled
2 cups heavy cream
4 egg yolks
1 whole egg
Salt to taste (about ¾ tsp.)
Freshly ground white pepper to taste

Heat oven to 350 degrees. Lightly oil six 3/4-cup ramekins and set aside, or prepare tamale tart pan.

Heat the olive oil in a skillet and add garlic. Sauté for 1 minute, then roast in 400-degree oven for 10–12 minutes (until soft and lightly browned). Place garlic in saucepan with cream and bring to a boil. Place in blender and purée garlic completely (about 1 minute) and pour into mixing bowl.

Beat egg and yolks together and whisk into garlic-cream mixture. Season with salt and white pepper and divide mixture between the six ramekins (mixture should come 3/4 of the way up sides) or fill tamale tart pan.

Place ramekins in roasting pan and pour boiling water halfway up sides of ramekins. Place waxed paper over ramekins and cover pan with foil so that it is airtight.

Bake in oven for 25–28 minutes or until just set. When custards are done, turn off oven and leave door ajar to keep warm.

FILET OF SALMON WITH CILANTRO, ANCHOS, AND ORANGE

Serves 4

1/2 cup chicken stock
2 cloves garlic
1 cup heavy cream
2 cups cilantro leaves
10 spinach leaves (about 1 cup)
1 tsp. lime juice
Juice of 2 oranges
1/4 cup butter, cut into pieces
2 tsp. ancho chile purée
3 tbsp. vegetable oil
4 salmon filets (3–4 oz. each, about 1/2-inch thick)
Flour for dredging
Salt to taste

Heat chicken stock, garlic, and cream in saucepan until boiling. Reduce heat and let simmer for 7–10 minutes. Add cilantro and spinach leaves to stock and cook for 1 minute. Purée ingredients from sauce in blender for 2 minutes. Strain into bowl, add lime juice, and season with salt. Set aside and keep warm.

In second saucepan, reduce orange juice over high heat until 3 tbsp. remain. Reduce heat and whisk in butter, piece by piece. Whisk in chile purée and season with salt. Set aside and keep warm.

In a large skillet, heat the 3 tbsp. oil until lightly smoking. Season salmon filets and dredge in the flour. Cook each filet for 1 minute per side.

Ladle the cilantro sauce onto 4 warm plates. Place a salmon filet on each plate. Pour orange-ancho sauce over each filet.

CHIPOTLE LAMB CHOPS WITH CREAMED CORN PUDDING AND THREE TOMATO SALSAS

Serves 4

3 tbsp. olive oil
1/2 sweet onion (such as Vidalia), chopped
1/4 carrot, chopped
1/4 stalk of celery, chopped
2 sprigs thyme
3 sprigs rosemary
1/2 cup dry red wine
3/4 cup reduced lamb or veal stock
2 tsp. chipotle chile purée
2 tbsp. butter
8 rib lamb chops, 1-inch thick each
Salt to taste
Creamed Corn Pudding (recipe follows)
Three Tomato Salsas (recipe follows)

Build a medium-hot fire with charcoal and aromatic wood.

In a saucepan over high heat, heat 2 tbsp. of the olive oil and sauté the onion, carrot, and celery for 1 minute. Add the thyme and one sprig of the rosemary and cook for 1 minute longer, stirring frequently.

Add the red wine and reduce to a glaze. Lower heat and add the stock and chile purée. Cook for about 3 minutes longer. Whisk in the butter and season with salt. Strain sauce and keep warm while grilling lamb chops.

Brush the chops with the remaining tablespoon of oil and season with salt. Toss remaining sprigs of rosemary on coals and grill chops for 2 minutes per side for medium-rare.

Serve with chipotle sauce, Creamed Corn Pudding, and Three Tomato Salsas.

Creamed corn pudding

1 tbsp. butter
5 ears corn
1/2 cup heavy cream
2 medium egg yolks
3 medium whole eggs
Dash ground cinnamon
4 tbsp. red bell pepper, diced
1 serrano chile, seeded and minced
1 tbsp. cilantro, chopped
2 tsp. pure maple syrup
Salt to taste
Freshly ground white pepper to taste

Preheat oven to 375 degrees. Spread the butter on a 9-inch baking dish and set aside. With a sharp knife remove kernels and scrape cobs to extract "milk" onto a large plate.

In a mixing bowl, beat together the cream, yolks, whole eggs, cinnamon, pepper, serrano chile, cilantro, and maple syrup. Add the corn pulp and mix. Season with salt and pepper and pour into the buttered baking dish.

Cover with foil and bake in center of oven for 25 minutes.

Three tomato salsas

Tomatillo salsa:

2 scallions, chopped
8 tomatillos, husked, cored, and cut in 1/4-inch dice
2 cloves roasted garlic
1 tbsp. chopped cilantro
2 serrano chiles, seeded and diced
1 tsp. lime juice
Salt to taste

Red tomato salsa:

4 small red tomtoes, seeded and cut in 1/4-inch dice
1/2 small red onion, peeled and diced
2 tbsp. red bell pepper, seeded and diced
2 cloves roasted garlic
1 tsp. lime juice
Salt to taste

Yellow tomato salsa:

4 small yellow tomatoes, seeded and diced (or 1 pt. yellow cherry tomatoes), seeded and cut in 1/4-inch dice
2 serrano chiles, seeded and diced
2 tbsp. yellow bell pepper, seeded and diced
3 tbsp. mango, diced
2 tsp. orange juice
Salt to taste

Procedure:
Combine ingredients for each salsa in three separate bowls. Let stand for at least 30 minutes.

WARM APPLE-RAISIN SPICE CAKE WITH CARAMEL SAUCE AND VANILLA ICE CREAM

1 cup cake flour
2 cups all-purpose flour
1½ tsp. baking soda
½ tsp. nutmeg
½ tsp. cinnamon
¼ tsp. ground clove
¼ tsp. mace
¼ tsp. powdered ginger
½ tsp. salt
1½ cups pure vegetable oil
2 cups granulated sugar
3 eggs
3½ cups raw chopped apples, unpeeled
¾ cup chopped roasted pecans
1 cup raisins, plumped in bourbon

Preheat oven to 325 degrees. Sift dry ingredients together except sugar. Set aside.

Beat oil and sugar in electric mixer at medium speed until light and fluffy (about 5 minutes). Add eggs, one at a time. Beat well. Gradually fold dry ingredients into sugar-oil mixture and combine thoroughly. Add apples, pecans, and raisins. Blend well with spatula.

Pour batter into a buttered and floured 10-inch springform pan. Bake for 1½ to 2 hours or until an inserted knife comes out dry.

Caramel sauce

⅓ cup granulated sugar
1 cup light brown sugar
¼ cup pure maple syrup
¼ cup dark corn syrup
1 cup heavy cream

Mix all ingredients in heavy-bottomed saucepan. Cook over high heat until mixture reaches 220 degrees on candy thermometer. Let cool for 20 minutes and skim surface if necessary. Drizzle over cake.

Vanilla ice cream (1 qt.):

2 cups milk
1 vanilla bean, split in half lengthwise and scraped
⅔ cup sugar
6 egg yolks
¾ cup heavy cream or creme fraiche

In medium saucepan, bring milk to boil with vanilla bean. Remove from heat and cover. Let infuse for 15 minutes. Meanwhile, add sugar to yolks while whisking. Continue whisking a few minutes until yolks have lightened in color.

Bring milk back to boil and slowly pour milk through strainer into yolks, while stirring. Discard vanilla bean.

Pour strained mixture back into saucepan and cook over low heat, all the while stirring with wooden spatula. Scrape sides and bottom and continue cooking until mixture reaches 185 degrees on candy thermometer and also has thickened considerably. Immediately remove from heat and place over ice. Stir in chilled cream or creme fraiche and let chill thoroughly. Place in ice cream machine and freeze.

Gert Rausch

Born November 24, 1946, in Blankenburg, Germany, Gert Rausch apprenticed in Germany and then worked for hotels in Switzerland, France, Italy, Canada, South America, and the United States. His food has received a number of gold medals in various countries; he was featured as a BBC television chef, and his skills have been recognized in the *New York Times* as well as major Texas newspapers.

He is proud of being honored by Les Amis d'Escoffier and participating in the television series "Great Chefs of the Southwest."

Among his favorite things are any kind of music, Christmas, Black Forest cake, comfortable kitchen shoes, preparing any kind of wild game, eating Choucroute Garni, reading, going to movies, swimming, and sailing.

Chef Rausch believes the most difficult preparation is to make the perfect soufflé. His worst culinary disaster was to have the wrong menu for a party of 300 people at a Cape Cod function.

"My most embarrassing culinary moment was when all our supplies were undercooked at a special banquet for the Chefs' Association Annual Banquet in Montreal. My best culinary moment was working with Anton Mossiman, now executive chef at the Dorcester."

Chef Rausch says he enjoyed cooking school and, as to a most fun event, "I think each day is fun, otherwise I'd give up the profession."

He recommends arrowroot for a roux as the best substitute.

His definition of junk food: mass-produced Mexican food and hamburgers. And yes, he eats both of them.

Aphorisms of Gert Rausch

1. Be honest to yourself.
2. The customer is always right.
3. There is no shortcut to good cooking; even the simplest thing should be done right. If you do it right, you made the best short-cut.
4. You live only once, so do the best with your life. You make your own destiny.

CHEF GERT RAUSCH

Austin's Courtyard
1205 North Lamar
Austin
(512) 476-7095

Menu

Black Bean Soup

Domaine Laurier Sauvignon Blanc or Louis Martini Pinot Noir

Gravlax

La Crema Chardonnay or Monticello Chevier Blanc

Gulfcoast Fish en Croute

Lyeth White Table Wine or Groth Sauvignon Blanc

Veal Medallions with Ragôt of Mushrooms

Château Montelena Chardonnay or Grgich Hills Cabernet Sauvignon

Crepes Flambé with Grand Marnier

Coffee

Schramsberg Brut

BLACK BEAN SOUP

Serves 10–12

4 cups black beans, washed
Cold water as needed
3 stalks celery
3 large onions, finely chopped
1/2 cup butter
1/2 cup finely chopped parsley
Rind and bone of 1 cooked, smoked ham
3 leeks, thinly sliced
4 bay leaves
1 tbsp. seasoned salt
1 tsp. freshly ground black pepper
1 cup dry Madeira wine
Pinch of cayenne pepper
Croutons, sour cream, or goat cheese (optional)

Soak the beans overnight in enough cold water to cover them, then drain. Add 5 qts. cold water and cook the beans over low heat for 1 1/2 hours.

In a soup kettle over low heat, sauté the celery and onions in butter for about 6–8 minutes or until tender. Add chopped parsley and cook the mixture, stirring 1 minute.

Gradually stir in the beans and their water. Add the rind and the bone of the ham (rind should be chopped in small pieces), leeks, bay leaves, seasoned salt, and pepper. Simmer the soup for 4 hours.

Remove and discard the ham bone and bay leaves. Force the remainder through a sieve. Mix the puréed beans with their broth in cuisinart, then add the madeira and cayenne. Heat and stir the soup and serve immediately with croutons, sour cream, or goat cheese. Garnish with fresh basil leaf.

GRAVLAX

1 salmon, extremely fresh
10 oz. salt
5 oz. sugar
Fresh dill weed
3 carrots, thinly sliced
1 leek, thinly sliced
1 small bunch celery, thinly sliced
1 lemon, thinly sliced
5 juniper berries
2–3 tbsp. black pepper
1 oz. gin

Mix and pour ingredients over salmon, wrap tightly, let sit in refrigerator for 15 hours.

Pour off sauce and cover fish with fresh milk for 15 minutes. Dry fish well and refrigerate. To serve, slice thinly.

GULFCOAST FISH EN CROUTE

Serves 6–8

6 lbs. of fish (preferably snapper from Gulf of Mexico)
Chopped chervil
Chopped tarragon
Salt and pepper to taste
2 thin sheets of pastry dough (puff pastry or brioche dough) to cover fish
Egg yolk
Melted butter or beurre blanc

Buy a nice, very fresh snapper, gut it carefully, and remove the skin without hurting the meat. Leave the head and tail intact. Cut the fish along the back to the backbone. In this long cavity, place fresh chervil and tarragon, salt and pepper, and close the fish. Do the same thing on the belly.

Next, roll out 2 thin sheets of pastry dough the length of the fish. Place the fish on top of one of the pastry sheets, cover it with the other sheet, and seal the dough by pressing all around the fish (preserving original shape) until completely enclosed. Cut away extra pastry with a very sharp knife, leaving enough to simulate the fins and tail (optional). Use remaining dough to simulate gills and the eye.

Glaze the dough by brushing with beaten egg yolk. Decorate the fish by pressing the dough with a little mold in a half-moon shape to reproduce the scales. This careful work demands much patience and a certain dexterity.

Place fish thus prepared on a cookie sheet in a 425-degree oven. When the dough is firm, reduce the heat to 350 degrees, so it cooks evenly (inside and outside) without burning the dough. It will take about an hour to cook.

To serve, place the fish on a long platter and carve in front of the guests. Accompany it simply with melted butter or beurre blanc.

Variation:
Before it is wrapped in dough, the snapper can be stuffed with this excellent lobster mousse.

1/2 lb. raw lobster meat
Coral (optional)
3/4 tbsp. salt
Freshly ground pepper (a turn of the pepper mill)
Dash of nutmeg
1 cup heavy cream
1/4 lb. pistachios
Truffles

In a mortar, pound the lobster meat. Add the coral seasoned with salt, a turn of the pepper mill, and the finely grated nutmeg.

Rub the lobster meat through a very fine sieve into a bowl. Set the bowl on ice and beat into the lobster 1 cup very heavy cream and then the pistachios and truffles.

VEAL MEDALLIONS WITH RAGÔT OF MUSHROOMS

Serves 4

4 medallions of veal (6 oz. each) or 8 medallions (3 oz. each); medallions are cut from the veal loin and are rather thick
Seasoned salt and freshly ground white pepper
Flour
2 tbsp. cooking oil
1/4 cup unsalted butter, cut into small pieces
1 shallot, chopped fine
1 small garlic clove, chopped fine
2 tbsp. brandy
1/4 cup demi-glacé
1/4 cup heavy cream
2 mushroom caps
3 morille mushrooms
2 shiitake mushrooms

With the palm of your hand, flatten veal slightly. Season with salt and pepper. Dust lightly with flour, shaking off any excess. In a heavy skillet large enough to hold the veal, heat the oil. Over very high heat, brown the veal medallions about 30 seconds on each side.

Discard oil, lower heat, and add the butter, shallot, and garlic to pan. Cook for 1–2 minutes. Pour in brandy and ignite it. Flame will only last a few seconds. Add demi-glacé and cream, all mushrooms, and continue cooking until medallions are medium-rare, about 4–5 minutes for 6-oz. medallion, 2-3 minutes for 3-ounce medallion. Season with salt and pepper. Serve immediately on heated plate with sauce spooned over.

CREPES FLAMBÉ WITH GRAND MARNIER

Yield: approximately 30–35 crepes

2 1/2 cups sifted flour
4 eggs, plus 2 egg yolks
Pinch of salt
1 tbsp. granulated sugar
2 cups milk
1/2 lb. unsalted butter, melted, plus extra butter
1/4 cup Grand Marnier
2 tbsp. confectioners' sugar

In a bowl, combine the flour, eggs, egg yolks, salt, and granulated sugar. Pour in the milk slowly, stirring, in order to get a smooth batter without any lumps; finally add the melted butter and the Grand Marnier.

Heat the crepe pan and pour in a full tablespoon of the batter. As soon as the crepe detaches from the pan, shake it and flip it, and cook the second side.

Slide the crepe onto a buttered ovenproof dish; sprinkle with confectioners' sugar, and brown the sugar under the broiler.

Serve the crepes basted generously with Grand Marnier and flame in front of the guests. Serve 3 or 4 crepes per guest.

Note: Since this batter is made with butter, there is no need to grease the crepe pan for each crepe. The thinner the crepes, the better they are.

Optional: Grated orange peel for sauce.

Andrew Thomson

Andrew Thomson was born May 14, 1947, in England. He apprenticed mostly in England, where he received his City and Guild Certificates. In the United States, he has been recognized with various honors including the Top Chefs of America Award. His most esteemed honor, however, is seeing Cafe Pacific full and all the customers happy.

During his training he had his most embarrassing culinary moment: "I boiled roasting chickens and they all fell apart."

His worst disaster has been trying to recreate Oriental dishes.

"My best culinary moments are when I create a new dish and it is enjoyed and appreciated by our customers," he says. "And times are most fun on a really busy Saturday night when everything goes well in the kitchen and all work well together with no problems."

Chef Thomson says the most difficult preparation is to work with new ingredients, to get used to the taste, and find out what they work best with and which dishes they enhance.

The chef's favorite things include his mom's fruit cake, creating new dishes, trying new and different dishes, New Year's Eve, and being called chef.

"I earned the name and I like it," he smiled.

Aphorisms of Andrew Thomson

1. Chefs should enjoy their work and strive to be good spirits.
2. The best shortcut is to use the right tool for the right job.
3. Lemon juice and ginger are the two most successful substitutes.
4. Be on good terms with yourself for there are always far greater and far lesser persons than you.
5. Nobody should sing or whistle in the kitchen as it disturbs spirits and causes cream to go sour.

CHEF ANDREW THOMSON

Cafe Pacific
24 Highland Park Shopping Village
Dallas
(214) 526-1170

Menu

Tortilla Salad with Vinaigrette

Sterling Sauvignon Blanc or Fall Creek Chenin Blanc

Roast Tenderloin of Lamb with Fresh Mint Concasse,
Wild Mushroom Compote, and Merlot Butter Sauce
or Cabernet Sauce

Shafer Cabernet and Shafer Merlot

Oriental Salmon with Vegetables
and Chardonnay Butter Sauce

Chalk Hill Chardonnay or Pine Ridge Merlot

Devil's Food Cake with White Chocolate Sauce

Coffee

Piper Sonoma Brut

TORTILLA SALAD

Serves 6

2 qts. assorted greens, rinsed and chilled (oak leaf, romaine, mache, and red leaf lettuces)
1/2 red sweet onion, cut in strips
5 oz. Monterey Jack with jalapeño, shredded
Vinaigrette (see recipe)
1 avocado, medium ripe, cut with melon ball tool
3 chicken breasts, boned, grilled or smoked, cut in strips
Red, blue and white corn tortillas, cut in strips, fried crisp (see note)
2 tomatoes, seeded and cut in julienne strips
1/2 cup cilantro leaves

In a large bowl, toss the lettuces with onions, cheese, and vinaigrette. Divide among 6 chilled plates.

Arrange the avocado, chicken, tortillas, tomatoes on top, then sprinkle with cilantro. Drizzle remaining vinaigrette on top.

Note: If red and blue corn tortillas are not available, use 2 white corn and 2 yellow corn tortillas, cut in strips and fried crisp. Salt lightly, if desired.

Vinaigrette:

1 garlic clove, minced
1 tbsp. Dijon mustard
1 tbsp. lemon juice
4 tbsp. balsamic vinegar
1 tsp. sugar
1/2 tsp. salt
1/4 tsp. white pepper
2 tbsp. red chile oil
1/2 cup extra virgin olive oil

ROAST TENDERLOIN OF LAMB

Serves 6

Fresh mint concasse

1 clove garlic, minced
1 shallot, minced
1 tbsp. extra virgin olive oil
3 tomatoes, seeded, peeled, and diced (firm tomatoes, red, yellow, or a combination)
2 tbsp. fresh chopped mint
Salt and pepper to taste

Heat the garlic and shallot in olive oil over medium heat to soften. Remove from heat and stir in tomatoes and mint. Season to taste with salt and pepper.

Wild mushroom compote

1 clove garlic, minced
1 shallot, minced
2 tbsp. clarified butter
12 domestic mushrooms, sliced
6 oyster mushrooms, sliced
8 shiitake mushrooms, sliced
1 tbsp. fresh basil
Salt and pepper to taste
Reserved lamb drippings from lamb recipe

Sauté the garlic and shallot in butter in a large skillet over a medium heat for 2 minutes. Add the mushrooms and sauté 4–5 minutes. Season with basil, salt and pepper. Whisk in about 2 tbsp. of lamb drippings.

Lamb

2 lamb tenderloins, trimmed
Coarse salt
Olive oil
Fresh minced garlic
Minced rosemary
Coarse ground black pepper

Preheat oven to 500 degrees. Rub the lamb with oil, herbs, garlic, and pepper. Place on a roasting pan and cook medium rare, about 12–15 minutes. Meanwhile, prepare the sauces. (Reserve the lamb drippings for the mushroom compote.)

Merlot butter sauce

1 tsp. minced garlic
1 tbsp. minced shallot
1 sprig thyme
1 small celery stalk
1 small piece carrot
1/2 cup reduced lamb stock
1/3 cup Shafer Merlot*
1 tbsp. balsamic vinegar
1/2 lb. unsalted butter
Salt and pepper

In a medium saucepan bring the garlic, shallot, thyme, celery stalk, carrot, lamb stock, wine, and vinegar to a boil. Boil to reduce by half. Reduce the heat and whisk in the butter in spoonfuls to make a smooth, creamy sauce. Strain and then season to taste with salt and pepper.

* For Cabernet Sauce, substitute 1/3 cup Shafer Cabernet

Slice the lamb for service and serve with Merlot and Cabernet sauces, Fresh Mint Concasse, and Wild Mushroom Compote.

ORIENTAL SALMON

Serves 4

Oriental dressing

2 tsp. dry mustard
1 tsp. grated fresh ginger
2 tsp. sugar
2 tbsp. lemon juice
3 tsp. sesame oil
$1^1/_2$ tbsp. soy sauce
1 tsp. hot chile oil (available in Oriental markets)
$^1/_2$ cup vegetable oil
$^1/_2$ tsp. salt
$^1/_8$ tsp. pepper

In a blender, mix mustard, ginger, and sugar. Add remaining ingredients and blend smooth.

Salmon

4 (6–8-oz.) salmon filets
Fresh lemon juice
Olive oil
Salt
Pepper

Brush the salmon generously with lemon juice and oil, then season with salt and pepper. Heat the grill to the highest setting. Grill 3–4 minutes per side, brushing with oil as necessary to prevent sticking.

Chardonnay butter sauce

2 tbsp. rice wine vinegar
2 tbsp. Chalk Hill Chardonnay
1 shallot, minced
1 sprig thyme
1 tsp. fresh ginger
$1^1/_2$ sticks unsalted butter

In a saucepan, boil the vinegar, Chardonnay, shallot, thyme, and ginger to reduce by half the volume. Reduce heat. Over low heat, whisk in the butter, in small amounts, to make a smooth and creamy sauce.

Oriental vegetables

1 cup (about) bok choy, sliced diagonally
12 snow peas, julienne cut
1 red bell pepper, julienne cut
3 stalks celery, julienne cut
2 leeks, julienne cut
1 cup tatsio
1 cup Napa cabbage stalk, thinly sliced
1 tsp. ginger, minced

Mix 4 parts Chardonnay Butter Sauce with the Oriental Dressing and set aside.

Sauté Oriental Vegetables in hot oil until tender crisp. Remove from heat and whisk in sauce combination. Arrange around the plate.

Put the salmon in the center and top with sauce.

DEVIL'S FOOD CAKE

1/2 cup water
1 1/2 tsp. baking soda
2 tbsp. creme de cocoa
1/2 cup unsweetened cocoa
1 3/4 cups granulated sugar
2/3 cup unsalted butter
2 large grade AA eggs
2 1/2 cups sifted flour
3/4 cup buttermilk
2 tsp. vanilla

Combine the water with baking soda and cocoas and set aside.

Cream together the sugar and butter until light and fluffy. Add the eggs one at a time and beat in thoroughly.

Sift the flour and add to the batter alternately with the buttermilk. Stir in vanilla and the cocoa mixture.

Butter and lightly flour 2 9-inch cake pans. Shake out excess flour. Divide the batter between the two pans and bake at 325 for 30–45 minutes, or until a cake test determines doneness. Cool on racks before icing.

Chocolate icing

12 tbsp. butter
8 oz. semisweet chocolate
2 oz. unsweetened chocolate
3/4 cup heavy cream
3 cups confectioners' sugar
2 tsp. vanilla

Combine the butter and chocolate in a double boiler over simmering water and heat until melted. Whisk in the cream, confectioners' sugar, and vanilla and beat until very smooth. The consistency should be smooth and spreadable. If too thick, add more cream. Ice between layers, sides, and top.

White chocolate sauce

6 egg yolks
1 tbsp. cornstarch
2 cups whipping cream, heated to scalding
1/2 cup sugar
2 cups half-and-half
6 oz. white chocolate, broken in pieces
2 tsp. vanilla

Combine the egg yolks, cornstarch, cream, and sugar. Beat well. Heat the half-and-half with white chocolate to a boil. Stir until white chocolate is melted. Add vanilla. Gradually whisk in warm egg yolk and sugar mixture, and continue to cook over medium heat, stirring constantly, until the custard coats a spoon.

Remove from heat and strain into a deep ceramic bowl. Place the bowl in cracked ice to cool, stirring occasionally. The sauce will thicken as it cools.

Presentation:
Serve slices of cake in a pool of White Chocolate Sauce, and garnish with fresh raspberries.

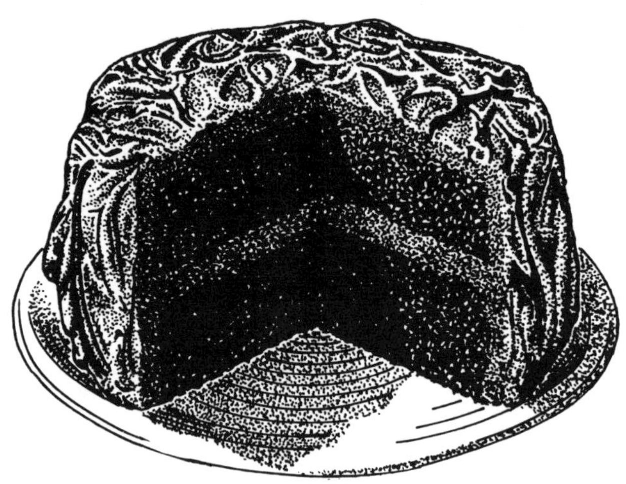

Wine Recommendations by Varietal Category

The wines I have suggested with the recipes frequently were selected from the restaurant wine lists; often they were not. My intention was to have the wines available at the restaurant if you chose to dine out rather than cook. Since wine lists change just as menus do, and in the event you cooked the chef's recipes at home, I wanted to recommend wines I've enjoyed with the same ingredients at other times. Also, for the most part, I selected moderately priced wines that would be available at markets as well as wine shops.

If your wine tastes happen to be identical to mine, you'll probably enjoy all the wines I've suggested, even though the bottles, and probably the vintages, will be different. Nonetheless, producers strive to present consistent styles, even though nature, bad corks, improper handling, and imperfect storage work equally hard to defeat the effort.

I encourage you to be adventuresome. Select several wines and taste each of them with every course. This approach will help you discover new pairings and expose you to new combinations. Your palate, and yours alone, is really the only valid judge of which wines and foods you match together. Train your palate and trust it.

CHENIN BLANC

Alexander Valley
Callaway
Fall Creek
Folie a Deux
Grand Cru
Hacienda
J. Lohr
Llano Estacado
Messina Hof
Preston
Simi
Ste. Genevieve

SAUVIGNON BLANC

Beringer
Buena Vista Fumé
Cakebread
Caymus
Château Souverain
Château St. Jean
Clos Pegase
Domaine Laurier
Dry Creek
Fall Creek
Ferrari-Carano Fumé
Grgich Hills
Groth
Hacienda
Inglenook
Iron Horse

Kendall-Jackson
Kenwood
Long
Lyeth White Table Wine
Matanzas Creek
Mondavi Fumé Blanc
Monticello Chevrier Blanc
(blended with Semillon)
Quail Creek
Sanford
Slaughter-Leftwich
Stag's Leap
Sterling

CHARDONNAY

Beringer
Burgess Cellars
Cambria
Chalk Hill
Château Montelena
Château Souverain
Chimney Rock
Christian Brothers
Barrel Fermented
Clos du Bois
Clos Pegase
De Loach
Domaine Michel
Eberle
Estancia
Fall Creek
Ferrari-Carano
Flora Springs
Hacienda Clair de Lune
Jekel
Jordan
Joseph Phelps
Kendall-Jackson
La Crema
Llano Estacado
Merryvale
Messina Hof Barrel Fermented
Morgan
Robert Mondavi
Simi
Slaughter-Leftwich
Sonoma-Cutrer, Les Pierres

CABERNET SAUVIGNON

Arrowood
Beaulieu
Beringer
Buena Vista
Cain
Caymus
Charles Krug
Clos du Bois
Conn Creek
Domaine Michel
Dominus
Fall Creek
Fisher
Franciscan
Freemark Abbey Bosche
Grand Cru
Grgich Hills
Haywood
Hess Collection
Jordan
Joseph Phelps
Laurel Glen
Llano Estacado
Lyeth Red Table Wine
Markham
Monticello
Oberhellmann
Opus One
Pheasant Ridge
Ridge
Rombauer
Sausal
Shafer
Silver Oak
Villa Mt. Eden

PINOT NOIR

Acacia
Beaulieu, Los Carneros
Bouchaine
Calera
Carneros Creek
Caymus
Etude
Gundlach-Bundschu
Hacienda
Iron Horse
Jaeger
Louis Martini
Navarro
Saintsbury
Stemmler

MERLOT

Benziger
Clos du Val
Duckhorn
Geyser Peak
Gundlach-Bundschu, Rhinefarm
Robert Keenan
Pine Ridge
Round Hill
Rutherford Hill
Shafer
Sterling

RIESLING

Freemark Abbey
Geyser Peak Soft J.R.
J. Lohr
Mirassou
Renaissance Dry White R.
Rodney Strong

GEWURZTRAMINER

Grand Cru
Sunny St. Helena

ZINFANDEL

Château Souverain
Rafanelli
Ravenswood

SPARKLING WINES

Culbertson Cuvee de Frontignon
Domaine Chandon Brut
Domaine Montreaux Brut
Domaine Mumm Brut
Gloria Ferrer Brut
Hanns Kornell
Iron Horse Brut
Jepson Brut
Korbel
Llano Estacado Brut
Maison Deutz Brut
Mirassou Brut
Moyer Brut
Piper-Sonoma Brut
Roederer Estate Brut
S. Anderson Brut
Scharffenberger Brut
Schramsberg Brut
Van der Kamp Brut
Wimberley Valley Brut

GAMAY BEAUJOLAIS

Beringer
Buena Vista

SEMILLON

Clos du Val
Oberhellmann

DESSERT WINES

Freemark Abbey Edelwein Gold Late Harvest Riesling
Grand Cru Late Harvest Gewurztraminer
Renaissance Late Harvest White Riesling

MISCELLANEOUS

Chalone Pinot Blanc
Consentino Crystal Valley Cabernet Sauvignon
Fall Creek Carnelian
Inglenook Charbono
Inglenook Gravion
Merlion Chevrier
Mirassou White Burgundy
Monticello Chevrier Blanc
Sanchez Creek Chambourcin
Val Verde Port
Wimberley Valley Cellar Select

GOOD VALUES (@ $6)

Beaulieu Burgundy
Christian Brothers Chenin Blanc
Christophe selections
Delicato selections
Ernest and Julio Gallo French Colombard
Glen Ellen selections
Llano Estacado Signature Red
Llano Estacado Signature White
M. G. Vallejo selections
Parducci selections
Villa Mt. Chenin Blanc
White Oak selections

BLUSHES

Christian Brothers White Zinfandel
Fall Creek Granite Blush
Llano Estacado Llano Blush
Simi Rose of Cabernet Sauvignon
Slaughter-Leftwich Austin Blush
Sutter Home

Glossary

al dente: firm pasta, not limp.

asiago: a table cheese made from cow's milk in northern Italy, Michigan, and Wisconsin and aged less than sixty days. When it is aged for long periods it makes an excellent grating cheese.

cilantro: leaf of fresh coriander.

concasse: coarsely chopped ingredients.

court bouillon: seasoned water for cooking fish, usually with various herbs and an acid (tomato, wine, vinegar, lemon juice).

forcemeat: pastes made of seafood or meat and bound with egg white and cream or butter and used as stuffings.

jicama: crisp tuber with a texture like water chestnut.

julienne: to cut in narrow strips lengthwise.

kasha: whole buckwheat groats.

keep warm: cover container with its own cover or with a clean towel after removing from burner.

lace fat: fat wrapped around meat to keep it moist.

masa harina: dehydrated corn flour used for tamales.

orzo: rice-shaped pasta.

ramekin: individual baking dishes of various sizes.

render: to reduce fat from meat by heating to melt and then drain off.

temper: to gradually raise the temperature of cold liquids by slowly stirring warm or hot ingredients into it.

tomatillo: resembles a small green tomato; remove brown tissue covering.

waterbath: placing a pan either in a larger pan or the sink filled with cold water that reaches beneath the rim of the pan in order to cool the mixture. Also used to cook custards by placing small containers in a pan filled with water to reach sufficiently under the rim of the dishes so as not to spill into the dishes.

CHILES (also known as capsicum, chili peppers, and peppers among other things): According to Anne Lindsay Greer in her book, *Cuis-*

ine of the American Southwest, "More chiles are produced and consumed than any other seasoning in the world. Chiles are named for their color, use, shape, place of origin or hotness. Confusion stems from the wide variety and the custom of changing the name as they turn red and are dried."

ancho: dried poblano chile.

ancho chile pods: the chile case.

chipotles: smoked, dark red, dried jalapeños, very hot.

jalapeño: approximately two-inch hot chile used in red or green stage.

pasilla: a dark brown (color of a raisin, *pasa* in Spanish), long, narrow, curved, mildly flavored variety. Dried, the pasilla resembles the ancho or mulato, which are often called pasilla mistakenly.

poblano: about half the size of a regular bell pepper; mild to medium hot dark green chile.

serrano: smaller than jalapeño; light green and very hot.

Thai chiles: Thailand exports large amounts of peppers; the Thai preference is for very hotly spiced foods.

STOCKS: Cooking at home is not the same as cooking in a professional restaurant kitchen. Equipment, products, and staff are just some of the differences. Frequently, ingredients are made daily and chefs have their bevy of kitchen helpers to prepare vats of stocks, vinegars, and glazes. In the home kitchen, at least in mine, making a good stock is a major three-day affair. First of all, chicken feet and veal knuckles are not on my daily grocery list; however, they are essential for a good homemade stock.

Stocks are basic and important ingredients for myriad recipes, especially sauces, gravies, and soups. Stocks are clear liquids derived from meat, fish, or fowl and their bones, or from vegetables. Water and bones are the major ingredients. Brown stock is made from beef and veal bones that have been browned; white stock from bones not browned, sometimes with chicken bones added. Fumet (fish stock) is made from the trimmings and bones of lean fish. Turkey, venison, and other game can also be used. Gelatin from the bones thickens stocks. Younger animals offer more of it. Cutting large bones into smaller pieces exposes more area for extraction. Adding meat gives depth to the stock.

General instructions:

Blanch the bones in order to prevent cloudiness in the stock. Rinse them in cold water, place them in a pot, and cover with cold water. Impurities rise to the surface as the water boils. Skim them off.

For *white stock,* remove and rinse the bones and place in the stock pot. Cover with cold water, heat to simmer, and add spices and herbs desired.

Skim the surface as needed; keep bones covered and simmer (seven hours for beef, three and a half hours for chicken, forty minutes for fish). When it's finished, cool the stock quickly in a waterbath in the sink, then cover and refrigerate or use. A workable ratio of ingredients is 100% water, 55% bones, and 10% herbs and spices.

For *brown stock,* do not blanch or wash the bones. Place a layer of bones in a pan and brown in a hot oven (385 degrees). It takes an hour to brown the bones sufficiently to give the stock color. Then cook as above.

Reductions are concentrated stocks. They're simmered to concentrate them.

Glazes are concentrated reductions created by further simmering until the mixture coats the back of a spoon.

A *demiglaze* is a rich brown sauce that reduces a glaze by one-half its consistency.

To *deglaze* a pan, put the liquid of your choice (water, wine, vegetable reduction, etc.) into the pan to dissolve the ingredients that remain in the pan.

Broth is the liquid that results from simmering chicken or beef or other comestibles.

A lot of good home cooks use their own recipes for stock. Stocks can also be bought in the form of canned and dried products or bouillon cubes.

MEASURES

1 ounce is 2 tablespoons (liquid)
8 ounces is 1 cup or 16 tablespoons (liquid)
32 ounces is 1 quart or 4 cups or $^{9}/_{10}$ of a liter (liquid)
1 liter is $4^{1}/_{3}$ cups (liquid) or 2.2 pounds

Index